Population studies, No. 40

The economically active population in Europe

Rossella Palomba and Irena E. Kotowska

Directorate General III – Social Cohesion

Council of Europe Publishing

b 2550 3509

The views expressed in this study are those of the authors and do not necessarily reflect those of the Council of Europe.

ZZ
CE
2003 E 11

Council of Europe Publishing
F-67075 Strasbourg Cedex

ISBN 92-871-5183-0
© Council of Europe, August 2003
Printed in Germany

Foreword

The Council of Europe has a long tradition of producing population studies, and the work of the European Population Committee contributes to the understanding of the relationship between social policy and demographic issues in Europe. The findings of this work are published in the series "Population studies", where topics covered include migration flows, national minorities, demographic changes and the labour market, the ageing of European populations and the demographic consequences of economic transition. These publications provide essential background information for implementing the Council of Europe's strategy for social cohesion: an integrated policy approach aimed at combating poverty and social exclusion through promoting access to social rights in areas such as employment and training, health, social protection, housing, education and social services.

The present volume examines two different aspects of the economically active population in Europe. In the first part, older workers in the labour market and retirement policies throughout Europe are analysed. The trend towards earlier retirement is looked at in the context of changing family structures, pension and social security systems and the greater flexibility of work patterns. Future trends are evaluated, particularly the possibility of increased activity rates among older people. The second part focuses on the reconciliation of working life and family life, an issue that is heavily gender-oriented as it is closely tied to the balance between paid employment and unpaid work taking care of the family. The report analyses changes in the workplace, such as technological innovations and the expansion of the service sector, and changes in family formation, all of which have led to more employment opportunities for mothers. The report also looks at welfare policies, including measures aimed at reconciling career development with family needs, childcare provision and changes to social benefits.

I should like to take this opportunity to thank the authors, Rossella Palomba and Irena E. Kotowska, for their work, which has resulted in the comprehensive and thorough study contained in this volume. My sincere thanks go also to the European Population Committee whose careful discussion of successive drafts has guaranteed the high quality of the final result.

Gabriella Battaini-Dragoni
Director General of Social Cohesion

Table of contents

Introduction

This volume in the "Population studies" series addresses the issue of active ageing in Europe. Part one examines the subject of the reconciliation of working life and family life and Part two explores the issue of older workers in the labour market and retirement policies.

Both parts discuss characteristics of the population in relation to labour force participation. The authors present a synthesis of available data and knowledge on the population at an economically active age. In line with the approach of the Council of Europe, the reports are not limited to western European countries; data on transition countries are also reported. This offers opportunities to enrich inter-European comparisons and it is hoped that it will generate still more standardisation of data-gathering and publication.

Both reports are focus-oriented. The terms of reference, drawn up by the European Population Committee, stated explicitly that the committee expected not only a review of available statistics, preferably a time series covering as many countries as possible, but also an argument that could be valuable for discussions in the committee, and throughout the Council of Europe member states, on social cohesion. The transformation of statistics and scientific knowledge into policy-sensitive arguments is not to be taken for granted: it requires an expert who is familiar with both scientific method and policy development.

The underlying reason behind the publication of these two reports in one volume relates to the application of a perspective on population that is well known to demographers and population scholars. The perspective is called the "life course" perspective. This longitudinal outlook describes and interprets life from a starting point to an end point. Some people live longer than others. From marriage/cohabitation to the birth of the first child, people live shorter or longer periods of time as couples without children. From entry into the labour market to retirement, people have shorter or longer careers.

The standard European career, or *Gestalt*, for a normal working life, covers the period between the first entry into the labour market and retirement at the legal retirement age. The period is dedicated to full-time work. Changes in the labour population during the last decades of the twentieth century urged social scientists to deconstruct this classical concept of working life which is said to be male-biased. Confronted with the increasing but discontinuous labour participation rates of women during their life course, the lifelong and full-time image of labour force participation no longer accurately described working careers. The same holds true for the decreasing retirement age. Here too, the normal working-life concept is challenged.

The deconstruction of an implicit concept of "working life" because it is not empirically accurate is one necessary step in building the knowledge substrata for labour market population analyses. Another necessary step is to map the political implications of this process. How is this gap between empirical facts and ideal conceptions to be interpreted? Is it a problem that the labour force becomes differentiated in terms of participation over the life course? Is the male working-life construct the only valuable benchmark for qualitative working lives? Is it a problem that half to two-thirds of Europeans in their 50s are no longer participating, or are participating less, in the labour market? For whom is it a problem and what problems are generated?

Some labour market sociologists are not convinced that – given the higher and longer participation of women in the labour market, and given the low mortality rates at activity ages – there is an urgent necessity to uphold the lifelong and full-time working life idea. They promote a more discontinuous concept of working life, where periods of higher involvement may be alternated with periods of lesser, or even no, involvement. The challenge is not to lose potential workers once and for all. In their view, longer working careers – even beyond the 65-year threshold – can be realised only when a person's labour force participation is really integrated with other life options. Family formation, parenting and caring for dependent relatives and others are one kind of option. Renewing skills is another option, not forgetting the appealing idea of travelling the world with partner and children. At the other end of people's working lives, preparing for new activities after retirement may be one of the reasons to slow down involvement somewhat. In short, these scholars are convinced that a more female-biased labour life course would bring about a higher quality of life and hence more motivated and less stressed workers.

But scholars who focus on the sustainability of the European social security system challenge this view. The ageing of the population is now recognised as the most important factor to be taken into account in developing labour market policies. How can we generate the necessary replacement incomes for the old and the oldest? How can we generate the incomes the social security system would give to those in a lesser or even no-involvement period of their working lives? Most of the European systems generate these incomes out of contributions from the labour force. There is indeed a problem. It seems that the concept of the discontinuous career presupposes a thorough rethinking of social security systems.

This view is also treated with scepticism by those authors who interpret discontinuous work histories as being flexible in favour of employers. In their view, flexibility is hardly ever in the interest of the employee. It gives rise to a modern form of slavery where employees are hired or dismissed according to the logic of the firm and therefore gradually lose more of their rights.

The European Population Committee agreed to study the reconciliation of working life and family life and older workers in the labour market and retirement policies from this perspective. It was convinced that bringing together figures and interpretations on both of these decisive moments in the working career would be beneficial to the discussions on these issues and their importance to social cohesion currently under way in all the member states of the Council of Europe. Indeed, social cohesion is not only a matter of material poverty and exclusion, it is also a matter of quality of life and of the social divisions behind well-being.

Professor Thérèse Jacobs
Centre for Population and Family Studies
Brussels (Belgium)

I. Reconciliation of work and family

Rossella Palomba

1. Setting the scene

The compatibility between work and family is an area of research that has relatively recently acquired scientific autonomy in the economic, sociological, psychological and demographic disciplines. Intimate relationships and daily interactions between household members are clearly influenced by the economic role of women and men on the labour market and the unpaid work activities carried out for the functioning of the family. Nevertheless, researchers have long tended to analyse these two spheres of life separately and to focus attention above all on the possible impact of female labour-force participation on family organisation and life. This dichotomy between work and family (or as recently and better put, work-life balance) arises from "underlying assumptions about men's and women's roles in family and paid work, assumptions that shape our workplaces as they shape all our social institutions" (Rapaport *et al.*, 2002, p. 1).

The current policies in this sector explicitly or implicitly involve this approach, according to which women and mothers have the task of solving the problems and any conflicts arising from the difficulties in reconciling personal and professional life. The concept of reconciliation between paid work for the market and unpaid work to take care of the family and children is therefore heavily gender-oriented, influenced by norms and stereotypes regarding men's and women's roles in society, and paying little attention to the problems of equality at the workplace and of equal career opportunities for women and men, who try to achieve something by commitments in both work and personal life.

The connections between work and family life are very complex. The picture is all the more complicated if we consider that both factors – work and family – undergo continuous changes. Adjustments between work and family, types of balances that can be found, and the conflicts that may unfortunately occur within couples and in the personal life of individuals are constantly changing. The state-of-the-art description in the field of work-family reconciliation will rapidly become outdated due to the changes taking place in the family and work situation. I will therefore limit this report to a more recent period of time and, in particular, the 1990s. Furthermore, many of my considerations are based on Community data and legislation.

The 1990s were years of major changes with regard to technological innovation and the market economy, which have had a major impact on families and the possibility of reconciling work and family. The increasing use of computers and mobile phones, for example, has allowed some people to work outside traditional places, for example, at home, in their car or in another city.

Furthermore, over the past decade the process of de-industrialisation and the resulting expansion of the service sector has led to profound changes in the labour demand in Europe, now characterised by procedures and times differing from the ones typical of the industrial society (Drew, 1998). In particular, European women have been appearing increasingly and in a more consistent manner on the labour market. In order to have an idea of the recent developments in this field, we need only recall that between 1994 and 1999 two thirds of the 6.8 million new jobs created in the European Union were assigned to women. The difference between men and women in employment rates thus fell to 19% in 1999, compared to 24.5% in the early 1990s (European Commission, 2000). Therefore the workplaces, work times and the structure of the labour force are changing and this can have an impact on family organisation.

Welfare policies, and in particular those designed to reconcile paid and unpaid work for the family, have been stimulated by these changes and are showing a greater concern for measures aimed at reconciling career with family needs or promoting a more equal sharing of family responsibilities between the partners in a way better suited to today's society (European Commission, 2001). Recent years have seen an increase in the provision of formal childcare for very young children, as well as maternity, paternity and parental-leave policies – though men still seem reluctant to take up their entitlements. At the same time, however, the need for a general reduction of welfare expenditure has produced the so-called "welfare retrenchment" (Pierson, 1994) which is not a mere playback or reversal of welfare-state development (Goldberg, 2001) and has involved "a significant increase in means-tested benefits (as opposed to universal benefits); a major shift of responsibility for social provision from the public to the private sector; and dramatic changes in benefit and eligibility rules" (Pierson, 1996, p. 157).

In this context, we should recall the demographic changes in the age structure of the population and in the timing of family formation. These developments are partly a response to more general economic, political and social change in the European continent and have partly acted as a catalyst in focusing the attention of politicians and economists on the future of the European populations and the need for changes in the market, in work organisation and in welfare systems to try to reduce the negative impact on public expenditure of the inevitable ageing of the population and of fertility decrease on the size of the labour force.

When we refer to reconciling paid work and family, we must, therefore, be dealing with a highly complicated situation, one which is continuously changing and which has considerable internal contradictions. As we shall see in this report, social, economic and demographic changes have influenced both the nature of family life and how families participate in the labour market. Labour-market changes have created greater flexibility and greater employment opportunities for mothers, but there is less job security and less fiscal support for families. The link between state, market and family has become more varied. Gender roles within both families and the workplace have become less sharply defined, but equality between men and women in the labour market and the home is still a "virtual reality" for many Europeans. These changes, and the ones in the welfare systems and in families, intersect with each other in a complex and diversified manner. The pathway leading to a work-life balance is therefore less clearly defined.

2. Social and family change

Do changes in family forms and recent demographic trends place new pressure on the need to balance work and family? Although the analysis of changes in European families and society is not the specific subject of this report, it is essential to interpret the transformations underway in this field and their possible impact on the reconciliation between work and family. In fact, while the changes in production processes, the labour market and welfare systems are all macro-factors that have an impact on people's personal work-family balance (whether they like it or not), demographic behaviour in the family field, such as the fall in fertility, may be interpreted as an attempt on the micro level to find a proper balance between working life and family organisation.

In contemporary societies, women obviously have greater opportunities for choosing how to "build" their personal life and to negotiate the commitments of the couple and the forms of household organisation they are involved in. It is also obvious that, although there are still significant gender differences with respect to employment and household organisation, the amount of freedom of choice in this respect and the range of possibilities that European women have today is infinitely greater than their grandmothers, and sometimes their mothers (Allan *et al.*, 2001).

It should also be considered that the period of childrearing has become longer[1] and postponed with respect to the age of the mothers, despite the fall in fertility rates of about 50% since 1960 (Carnoy, 1999). This trend to postpone maternity several years after the start of a woman's working life may also depend on the need to find a better compromise between work activities and procreation choices. The desire for economic independence by European women therefore tends to induce the postponement of family

13

formation, which in turn is considered to be one of the factors of the fall in European fertility. We should in any case be very prudent in linking these two factors. In fact, the low number of children could be one of the reasons motivating women to work outside the home, or the need to work can induce a reduction in the number of children, leading us to hypothesise the existence of a driving force behind both trends. The latter possibility is supported by evidence from several countries experiencing improvements in fertility rates, despite very high and still increasing female labour-force participation (Table 2.1).

Table 2.1 – Total fertility rates (TFR) and female employment rates in the EU countries, around 2000

Country	TFR	Female employment rates
Ireland	1.89	53.2
France	1.89	54.8
Luxembourg	1.78	50.0
Netherlands	1.72	63.4
Denmark	1.76	72.1
Portugal	1.54	60.4
United Kingdom	1.64	64.5
Belgium	1.65	51.9
Finland	1.73	65.2
Sweden	1.54	69.7
Spain	1.22	40.3
Greece	1.30	41.3
Austria	1.32	59.7
Italy	1.24	39.3
Germany	1.34	57.8

Social scientists have often noted that women and men are increasingly reluctant to make decisions that have long-term consequences and clearly limit their future freedom of choice. A child represents a significant and prolonged limitation on the individual's freedom of choice, above all for working women, since the presence of very young children requires a consistent time commitment by the mothers, which is difficult to reconcile with a full-time job (Bernhart, 1993). In the light of these considerations, responsible prospective parents may decide not to have children or not to have them yet if they are not absolutely sure they can organise family life in the best way, making it compatible with working life.

From the family point of view, the European demographic scenario is undergoing a great change. I believe that the two main trends changing the morphology of families and relevant with respect to the reconciliation between work and family are the gradual increase of non-marital living situations and of the marriage instability, as well as, of course, the reduction of the family size due to the fall in fertility, as already mentioned.

Unmarried cohabitation has now entered into various stages of the process of change in the partnership behaviour among Europeans – above all in northern and central Europe – in the form of premarital cohabitation and as a stable non-marital union or as a particular stage of life for many young people, that is youth unmarried cohabitation, involving a less formal framework in the commitment between partners (Manting, 1996; Giddens, 1991, 1992). This form of union is no longer an obstacle to the birth of children. As a matter of fact, the number of children born out of wedlock is rising. According to the family fertility survey, 58% of young Swedish women born in the early 1960s lived in unmarried cohabitation at the birth of their first child. This rate is 30% for the Austrian women of the same birth cohort, 27% in France,[2] 17.7% in Finland, and 14.7% in Slovenia. In the UK, 40% of children are born out of wedlock and above all from cohabiting couples (Hardy, Adnett, 2001).

The other important trend in the European family scenario is the increase of families resulting from the dissolution of marriages, above all due to the economic problems involved and to the poverty risks run by the families of lone mothers. Marriage stability has decreased in all the European countries. Between 1970 and 1980, the divorce rate doubled in Belgium, tripled in France and the Netherlands and quintupled in the UK (Goode, 1993; Rendall et al., 2001). It has been estimated that in northern Europe about one marriage out of three will end in a divorce (Prinz, 1995). In the Catholic countries, the divorce rate is lower, but still rising (Allan et al., 2001). In any case, women are no longer forced to remain in an unsatisfactory union for economic reasons or for the lack of a personal income. What consequences does this have with regard to reconciliation between work and family?

Divorce triggers a revolution in the life of individuals. It thus implies the development and strengthening of policy measures to support lone-mother families, and raises important issues regarding the relationship between men, women and society through childrearing (Holden and Smock, 1991; Orloff, 1993). Divorce is, in fact, a decision taken by spouses that, besides having consequences on minor children who are specifically protected in all

1. The prolonged stay of children in their parents' home is a very major aspect of family change, above all in the southern European countries (Fernandez Cordòn, 1997; Menniti, Misiti, 2000)
2. For France, the birth cohort considered is the one between 1959-1963; for Finland, 1953-1957.

the European countries, also puts many lone-mother families in a position of economic weakness, thus requiring public support and plans for job insertion for those women who have never worked. In many European countries except the UK, the Netherlands and Germany, lone mothers have more paid work than married or cohabiting mothers (Bradshaw *et al.*, 1996) and the growing number of lone-parent families has provided a further stimulus to family-friendly working practices. Obviously, these elements do not consider all families after a divorce or separation and we should avoid generalising any possible consequences of the dissolution of marriage regarding the economic independence of the family. However, there is no doubt that the increase of lone mothers and children born out of wedlock has stimulated policy responses above all for the protection of those groups of the population that are weaker and poorer, or that are at risk of social marginalisation.

In any case, it is also true that if we look at the family changes in the context of the work-family balance, we can see that the new trends are almost always accompanied by the presence of women and mothers in the world of work. There is a relationship between new forms of family life and female employment, although it is not simplistic, in the sense that in the new families the status of lone parent or partner of an informal union is almost always associated with working women or mothers, although this is not the factor determining the new forms of union or the dissolution of marriages. Nevertheless, there are often working mothers in these circumstances.

Very briefly, we can see that from the demographic point of view, there are trends with opposite consequences with regard to the reconciliation between work and family. The increasing postponement of the formation of the family and the fall in fertility rate are factors that should make it easier to find a balance between work and family life. On the other hand, however, there are trends towards the de-institutionalisation of unions and instability of marriages that challenge the traditional form of families with the man as breadwinner (or half-breadwinner), and involving the need (if the desire was not already present) for the woman to have complete economic independence. Thus, there are complex relationships between the growth in paid female employment and the diffusion of new demographic and family behaviour, making it difficult to identify the direction of the change from the viewpoint of the work-life balance. The traditional view of the problem according to which married women should face problems of home and family organisation and management as well as having a job, must in any case be reviewed in the light of the changes under way.

3. Welfare and the work-life balance

Among the various political and social considerations aimed at improving family and labour policies in the EU in recent years, one of the most important considerations has been the attempt to promote a greater participation by women in the labour market. In fact, despite the widespread increase of unemployment in all the European countries, governments are trying to increase female employment as a means to produce greater opportunities for social inclusion, to reduce the dependence of families on welfare systems, and in the long term to counter the fall of the labour force due to the decrease in fertility. If we consider the EU as a whole, achieving the average target of female employment of 60% would bring an additional 10 million women into employment (Hardy, Adnett, 2001). This potential increase of the labour force, which is so important in the light of the increasing demands on the welfare system due to population ageing, has encouraged governments to intervene in favour of working women, also with the aim of broadening the base of contribution payers.

While the female employment rate has doubled over the last fifty years in many countries, there remain large differences within the EU with national female employment rates currently ranging from 72% to 40%. Denmark, Finland, the Netherlands, Portugal, Sweden and the United Kingdom already have female employment rates in excess of the 60% target, though Italy would have to increase its female employment by 37% and Spain by 38% to achieve the target (European Commission, 2001).

Employment rates of the mother generally fall after maternity. Nevertheless, greater participation in the labour market by mothers of children between 0 and 4 years has contributed to the increase of female employment in Europe (OECD, 2001). Also in this field, there are major differences between countries in the employment rates of the mothers and in the choice between full-time or part-time work.

The central European countries (Czech Republic, Hungary and Poland) deserve a particular mention. They were independent from the Soviet Union when the Berlin Wall fell, despite the close trade links, and have now gone over to a market economy, with reasonably competent state institutions. Social transfers increased relative to Gross Domestic Product (GDP) or remained constant. The economies of the Baltic states, after an initial period of crisis, have recovered and in any case the functioning of state institutions has remained reasonably efficient and credible, guaranteeing rights for work-ing mothers and women. This has not been the case in the former Soviet republics where, with the decreasing number of childcare facilities, many women have been forced to abandon work (O'Reilly, 1996).

In any case, as long as the changes in active participation in the world of work fail to bring about an immediate increase in gender inequality in European societies, policies must be implemented to adequately support paid work and childrearing (Lewis, 2001).

3.1. The current EU legal framework

The current family policies in all the European countries have the primary aim of achieving the conditions for mothers to raise their children through two basic instruments: a) periods of leave from work for mothers before and after the birth of the child; b) assistance to very young children through childcare facilities such as crèches and kindergartens, to enable the parents to do paid work. These forms of leave from work have recently been extended to fathers in many European countries. However, it should be noted that up to now women are the main and usually the only beneficiaries of statutory childcare leave.

Although the European Commission has no direct competence in the area of family policy, it has increasingly turned its attention to examining and understanding the social and economic implications of new trends in society on families and it has undertaken several initiatives aimed at reconciling work and family life. The Commission gave its opinion on the topic of work-life balance, pursuant to Article 13, introduced by the Treaty of Amsterdam, giving the possibility to build a legal framework to counter discrimination "based on gender, racial or ethnic origin, religion or belief, disability or age or sexual orientation."

The main portion of recent EU legislation on the work-life balance is the Parental Leave Directive of 1996 (96/34/EC, OJ L-145/4). In order to hasten social progress[3] in the field of the work-life balance, this directive was again approved by a unanimous vote in December 1997 and was implemented across the EU by 15 December 1999 (15 December 1997, OJ C-30/1 and 22 February 1999, OJ C-69/2 respectively). In terms of reconciling work and family life, the directive reads:

> "Policies on career breaks, parental leave and part-time work, as well as flexible working arrangements which serve the interests of both employers and employees, are of particular importance to women and men. Implementation of the various directives and social-partner agreements in this area should be accelerated and monitored regularly. There must be an adequate provision of good-quality care for children and other dependants in order to support women's and men's entry and continued participation in the labour market. An equal sharing of family responsibilities is crucial in this respect."

The main objective of the Parental Leave Directive is to enable workers with very young children to reconcile the care of their children with their parental and professional responsibilities. This priority objective affirmed by European

---

3. We can recall that a directive has the task of setting the objectives to achieve. Each country must implement adequate measures to achieve the agreed results.

social policies also contains an explicit reference to the fact that a greater participation of women in the labour market is not only crucial for the long-term economic interests of the EU, but also to favour greater social justice (Article 1).

In this regard, the Parental Leave Directive lays down some basic rules, such as the principle that this legislation is applicable to all workers. In terms of rights, men and women are entitled to three months of leave for the birth or adoption of a child in order to "look after a child or to make arrangements for the good of the child." Furthermore, the directive suggests that this period may be added to maternity leave. Such leave applies to both parents and those who have acquired parental responsibility and is applicable until the child is 8 years old (except with disabled children where the applicability extends until the age of 18). During such leave, an employee's contract will continue but neither pay nor any other benefits apply. For instance, pensions will be frozen. At the end of the leave, the employee has the right to return to the same or equivalent job consistent with his/her contract of employment. All social security implications are to be determined according to national law.

Among the fifteen EU member countries, about half have a form of unpaid leave. In the others, there is a combination of means and non-means-tested benefits. The duration of the leave varies from three to thirty-six months and according to the flexibility of use, since in some countries it must be taken near the birth of the child. In other countries, it can be used upon the discretion of the parents. A recent study conducted in the EU countries (Moss, Deven, 2000) shows that Sweden is the most advanced country in this field with fifteen months of leave, thirteen weeks per parent, usable in blocks of four weeks per year, until the child reaches the age of 8. Parental leave is taken by 70% of fathers, an exception in the European panorama that may be due to various factors. The fact that parental leave was introduced in Sweden over a quarter of century ago, with the aim of promoting the work of the mothers, has certainly made the practice part of the culture of that country.

The directive represents progress in reconciling work and family responsibilities because in establishing the period of leave it also indicates the basic principles to be adopted by national legislators, although it is unclear how all this could contribute to achieving greater equality on the job and a more equal sharing of housework, as indicated in the directive. In any case, there is a lack of reliable data on the use of parental leave and many countries, for various reasons, are unable to supply information on this subject (EC, 1998). This lack of information prevents us from actually measuring the impact of the policies on families and even more so from assessing the reconciliation of work and family life.

We can in any case note a gradual increase in the degree of "convergence" between European countries in the field of maternity and parental leave, and the differences between countries are decreasing. The changes in the types of maternity and parental leave "have brought closer countries belonging to different models of family policies" (Fotakis, 2000). For example, we can cite the UK, which since 15 December 1999 is no longer a perfect example of the non-interventionist liberal model in the family field, since it has introduced parental leave for thirteen weeks usable until the child reaches the age of 5. The attempt of the European Commission to find "windows of opportunity" and its pressure to seek new and positive developments in the field of the work-life balance of individuals, women and families seems to have had positive results.

3.2. Career breaks

Social policies can affect women's decisions regarding having children in different ways. On the one hand policies facilitate the work and motherhood combination by reducing the costs of care, by providing quality services, legal protection against firing and against discriminatory practices regarding hiring mothers; on the other hand policies give advantages to non working parents: by giving tax or cash extra advantages in case of a non working spouse with children or by providing replacement income in case of career breaks, implicitly encouraging women to leave the labour market when the children are very young. In fact, some policies aimed at facilitating the combination between work and family life, like parental leave and other forms of career breaks, that are taken nearly exclusively by women, decrease the growth of female labour force and *de facto* encourage women to stay at home (Bettio, 1998).

Economic considerations evidently play a large part in the decision to take a career break. However, sometimes parents have no choice but to have a period off work for the time it takes to give birth to and bring up children. Mothers are much more likely than fathers to exercise the right to career interruptions (Bruning and Plantenga, 1999) and as a consequence be more likely to be placed on the "mummy track" with lower career prospects (Hardy and Adnett, 2001). We are obviously referring to policies entitling parents (or better women) to the right to be off work for a limited period of time and not to the withdrawal from work on a voluntary basis, which is always possible.

The EU Commission's Report on equal opportunities for 2000 (2001) acknowledges that the policy emphasis has been on targeted active labour market policies and promoting a family-friendly work environment to raise female employment rates. There is a wide range of differing approaches to transposing an EU family-friendly initiative amongst individual member states. As a consequence "the EU notion of family-friendly has become more individualised and restricted by differences in the trade-offs made between social and economic rights at the national level" (Hardy and Adnett, 2001, p. 22). Female employment has developed unevenly in the EU. Differences in flexible working patterns together with diverse demographic trends and social, cultural and workplace norms affecting the relative power and autonomy of women, suggest the need for minimum floors rather than a levelling-up of social protection in this area. A common policy would be unlikely to produce uniform changes or even convergence given these underlying differences in contextual factors.

Existing career break schemes around the birth of a child are very illuminating under this perspective. In many cases, the schemes are of a general type and the birth of a child is one of the possible events. In Belgium, a wide range of measures for rearranging and redistributing working hours were introduced during the 1990s. One feature of this has been the career break schemes, which Belgium has pioneered together with Denmark (Meulders et al., 1999). One of the aims of this form of suspension of the contract of employment was to share out available employment. The intention is that employees (with at least six months' length of service) give up working for a specified period and, provided they are replaced by other workers, receive compensatory payment from the government. This arrangement must be agreed between employer and employee. If they wish to be eligible for compensation under this scheme, employees have to submit their application in writing three months before the start of the suspension, which lasts for no less than six months and no more than one year. The employees in question must be replaced by wholly unemployed workers currently receiving unemployment benefit. Compensation can also be paid to full-time employees who agree with their employer to change over to working only half-time, provided they are replaced by unemployed workers. Employees whose contract of employment is suspended under this career break scheme enjoy special protection against dismissal. The possibilities under the career break schemes have been broadened by means of new types of part-time career breaks and the introduction of arrangements benefiting the employer, whereby his contributions are reduced to compensate for the extra expense involved in taking on a replacement; the maximum duration for a career break in the public sector has also been extended. The minimum duration of a career break has been reduced to three months (from six months). In the public sector, employees have the right to a career break; the maximum duration of a career break has been changed to six years. There is a limited right to a career break in the private sector. The arrangements for part-time career breaks have been broadened: working time may by reduced by one-fifth, one quarter, one-third or half of normal full-time working hours. In addition, protection against dismissal, which already existed for workers taking a full-time career break, has been extended to cover workers taking a part-time career break. Employers are granted a reduction in their social security contributions for a worker replacing another worker on a career break.

Denmark as well has introduced a successful practice of career breaks whereby employees take one year's break from work, to be replaced, preferably, by an unemployed person. This policy has led to a type of work rotation, which has allowed unemployed persons to rejoin the workforce, and which subsequently improves their chances for further employment. Under the scheme, longer term qualified unemployed people are given preference to replace those seeking career breaks.

The recent strong economic performance of the Irish economy has been associated with a rapid rise in female employment that has now reached the EU average. Although Ireland shared with the UK a reluctance to use legislation to restrict employment at will, Ireland's 1998 Parental Leave, 1997 Working Time, and 1998 Employment Equality Acts now provide a floor of statutory rights relating to work-life balance issues. Irish law gives each parent fourteen weeks unpaid parental leave per child until the child is 5. The career break is well established in the public sector. The system allows civil servants to take special unpaid leave (minimum six months, maximum five years) to bring up children or for other domestic reasons, training or travel abroad. Civil servants wishing to return to work after a career break are assigned to the first available vacant post, with a guarantee that they will be re-employed within twelve months.

In the Netherlands the idea is to create a financial incentive for working people to take a period of leave. In this proposal a possibility (no legal entitlement) is given to employees to take leave for care or educational purposes. The duration of the career break is a minimum of two and a maximum of six months. The person replacing the employee on leave can also be employed elsewhere in the organisation. The appraisal of the way the Career Break (Funding) Act operated showed that only modest use has been made of the act. The main obstacles are lack of familiarity with the scheme and the replacement requirement (that is that someone belonging to one of the specified groups of benefit claimants should replace the person going on leave). The government is proposing improvements in both areas.

The career break ends with a return to either full-time or part-time work. All those who had taken career breaks had regrets as far as their career was concerned and felt that the interruption had disadvantaged their career progression (OECD, 1994). Leaving employment for a few months, or even a few years, may result in a gap in the career of most women and time away from the workplace can be disruptive and people re-entering the workforce often feel intimidated by the changes that take place, even over a short period.

Two interesting additional conclusions were drawn by Colin (1995) with regard to earnings comparisons. Earnings were found to be lowered for the individuals who experienced career breaks in comparison with the ones who did not, and the decrease in earnings observed for the individuals who had incomplete careers (in comparison with the ones who had continuous careers) is higher for women, who also experience the longest career breaks. As a final consideration, if an employee takes a career break this might hamper his/her rights to a supplementary pension, or he/she might find that they are not fully-indexed thus losing out in comparison with his/her fellow employees.

In no European country do women have *de facto* the same opportunities as men to combine an economically active life and a family. Women of every generation carry the main responsibility for the care of children and other dependant persons. If they take career breaks to look after the children, it is highly probable that they will face problems in re-entering the job market, in the level of their salaries and in their pension levels.

3.3. Childcare services

In the years to come, the growing demand for services intended for families with very young children will rise together with the increase in the presence of working mothers, thus representing a major challenge for European societies and policy-makers. This demand at the national level must, however, take into account the retrenchment under way in the European welfare systems.

A comparative study conducted in nine European countries[4] on the changes in the welfare system in the late 1990s (Goldberg and Rosenthal, 2001) has shown that what is called welfare-state reform is, in general, a euphemism for retrenchment from the economic viewpoint. In particular, in the eight countries where data are available, we can see an increase in expenditure on the elderly and the disabled – not necessarily proportional to the increase due to the rise in the percentage of elderly people in the population – but six of the countries examined recorded a fall in overall family-friendly investment both in terms of cash benefits and of family services; only France and Germany increased expenditure for families at the end of the observation period (Table 3.1).

---

4. Canada, France, Germany, Hungary, Italy, Japan, Sweden, United Kingdom, and USA.

Table 3.1 – Percentage changes in social expenditure for selected social programmes, 1980-1995

Country	Health	Old age cash	Unemployment	Family cash	Family service	Total expenditures on families	Elderly/ disabled services
Canada	26.8	55.6	6.6	25	-27.3	-2.3	
France	34	33	36.6	-4.5	27.6	23.1	23.8
Germany	16.8	3	200	-33.5	50	16.5	75.8
Italy	-4.6	49.3	45	-56.5	-16.7	-73.2	5.3
Japan	22.4	56.9	18.1	-13	-12	-25	92.9
Sweden	-31.9	19.6	489.7	19	-25.5	-6.5	91.5
UK	17.2	27.4	-16	5.6	-7.7	-2.1	28.3
USA	64.4	6.1	-49.3	-28.3	-8.8	-37.1	-61.5

Source: Goldberg, and Rosenthal, 2001.

The main trend is to increase selectivity and means-tested benefits. For example, in Sweden, which has always been the country in Europe best symbolising a quality childcare system extensively financed by the government, over the past fifteen years there has been an increase in the fees for children using the service and an increase in the number of children per childcare worker both in day-care centres and in afternoon-school programmes. This is why there is a widespread feeling among users that the quality of the service has worsened (NBHW, 1997). Furthermore, there is a greater variability of municipal services and a trend without precedent in Sweden towards selectivity – as opposed to universality – in the eligibility criteria for the use of childcare services. In particular, children with an unemployed parent are excluded from using the public childcare service, although perhaps these children need it most (Lachs, Ginsburg and Rosenthal, 2001).

Goldberg and Rosenthal (2001, p. 342), on the basis of the results of their analysis concerning welfare in nine European countries, conclude: "we have not heard the rhetoric of retrenchment in welfare-state systems but perceive the reality of it". All this affects the practical possibility for families and mothers to adequately reconcile the requirements of life and work. While with regard to rights, which are basically freedom, social cohesion and European democracy, which are set forth at the Community level, no retreat is likely with regard to family services, but when decisions are left to the individual states, this may be possible in terms of the increasing privatisation of the services and of the narrowing of the eligibility criteria for the use of such services.

Table 3.2 – Percentage of children in publicly funded childcare and education institutions by age of children, 1993

Country	< age 3	Age 3 to school age
Austria	3	75
Belgium	30	95
Denmark	50	79
Finland	27	43
France	23	99
Germany	5*	65*
Greece	3	64
Ireland	2	52
Italy	6	97
Luxembourg	2*	68
Netherlands	8	69
Portugal	12	48
Spain	5	84
Sweden	33	79
UK	2	53

*: 1988 data.
Source: Gauthier, 2000: The data comes from the European Commission network on childcare. It covers children in pre-primary schools, day-care centres, kindergartens, crèches, and family daycare, as long as the service was partly or fully publicly funded.

We should also consider that the data on the availability of childcare services and the possibility of international comparisons on this topic involve many problems. We need only recall that the most recent data dates to almost ten years ago and certainly cannot reflect the profound changes that have taken place recently. In any case, it is useful to look at the situation in the EU countries, which, although not updated, nevertheless gives an idea of the national differences (Table 3.2).

Over 90% of children aged between 3 and school age attended publicly financed childcare institutions in Belgium, France, and Italy, while lower percentages of 60% are recorded in Finland, Ireland, Portugal, and the UK. The percentages for children aged under 3 are definitely lower and only Denmark shows 50% of children aged from 0 to 3 enrolled in publicly financed childcare institutions (Gautier, 2000).

There are also alternative forms of childcare with respect to the traditional type. These forms should be considered insofar as they seek to satisfy the specific needs of specific families. In any case, what is suitable for one family may not be suited to another. For example, in Finland (Taskinen, 2000) families have various options. Parents can choose to look after the child themselves with the help of the child home-care allowance, or they can place their child in a day-care centre run by the municipal authorities. It is also possible to choose the private day-care allowance and arrange for childcare privately in a private nursery or have a nurse at home. These different approaches can produce differences in the utilisation of public services.

With regard to the eastern and central European countries, economic transfers to families in terms of social benefits and family allowances (among these large families, lone-parent families, etc.) and services were an essential part of their family policies before the economic changes occurred, subsequent to the fall of the Berlin Wall, and family-friendly measures were greater with respect to those in western Europe. Only France and the Scandinavian countries have always enjoyed benefits comparable with those in the countries of central and eastern Europe.

These countries have undergone general erosion in the value of the support and services to families with children, due to a decline in government expenditure and with the introduction of substantial user-fees. The real value of social transfers has been eroded for all social groups (O'Reilly, 1996). The decentralisation of social services has also had negative effects on services and in general on support to families, since the local authorities often have too few resources to maintain the previous levels. The number of crèches and kindergartens has been reduced and consumer fees have been introduced, leading to the loss of the universality of the service and the exclusion of many children from this opportunity. Maternity leave, childcare leave, child allowance and child support are still funded by the central and eastern European governments, but there is debate on whether to maintain the universality of these benefits and to what degree they are to be index-adjusted to limit public expenditure.

It is interesting to note the trends in the preferences expressed by the populations of various countries towards the services to better reconcile work and family. In this field, the best source is the PPA-population policy attitudes and acceptance survey conducted in the 1990s in various European countries.[5] The survey, of which the second round is now under way, shows that the preferences of Europeans vary according to their family status and to other characteristics (Table 3.3).

---

5. The survey conducted in the early 1990s covered nine European countries: Austria, Belgium (Fl), the Czech and Slovak Republics, Germany, Hungary, Italy, the Netherlands, Spain and Switzerland.

Table 3.3 – Childcare facilities and policies to promote a better combination of work and family by some characteristics of the respondents (% in favour or strongly in favour)

Characteristics of the respondent	Better care facilities for children under 3 years of age	Better care facilities for children between 3 and school age	Part-time for parents with young children	Flexible working hours for parents with young children	Better work opportunities for parents with young children
Sex					
Male	89	81	80	84	86
Female	92	84	87	90	92
Living arrangement					
Single	89	86	77	82	84
Lone parent	88	93	92	89	91
Partner, 1-2 children	90	84	87	89	90
Partner, 3+ children	85	83	89	85	88
Employment situation					
Double income, wife: full-time	86	92	86	87	91
Double income, wife: part-time	85	86	77	85	84
Sole income, wife: housewife	90	62	81	85	84
Number of children					
No children	92	80	79	87	88
1	91	87	89	90	90
2	89	83	87	85	88
3+	91	82	89	85	88
Total	91	82	84	87	89

Source: Nebenführ, 1998.

In general, we can say that in the PPA study all the measures proposed have met with a high level of acceptance. The respondents working full-time and with children saw the possibility of having better childcare services as the most appropriate strategy for their work-life balance. On the other hand, those working part-time and with children favoured primarily the extension of the possibility of part-time work as the best strategy for reconciling work and family. Services for children are also very much requested by those who have no children and perhaps this is one of the reasons preventing them from having children (Nebenführ, 1998).

In any case, a comparison between the European countries shows that the lowest fertility rates are often associated with countries with greater differences between men and women with respect to employment (Table 3.4). If higher fertility can be considered as an indirect indicator of better conditions of compatibility between work and family life, the modernisation of gender roles through policies oriented towards gender equality on the labour market could create the most appropriate opportunities for work-life balance. In any case, these differences between countries also show that a common policy (for example Community policy) towards the integration of women into the labour market will not produce the same effects everywhere, at least in the short term.

There are, in any case, few studies focusing on the impact of family policies on the participation of women in the labour market. As Gauthier (2000), very rightly observes, "the lack of outcome studies may partly be explained by a lack of appropriate data." This is obviously the cultural gap which should be promptly bridged, otherwise the analysis of the services available to families and the effectiveness of the measures in terms of female employment and work-family balance will continue to lack the necessary links of communication and interpretation ability.

Any attempt to measure the impact of public policies on family life and mothers' employment requires redefining the traditional approach of family policies. This is especially true in relation to the increasingly uncertain boundaries in the field of family policies and other policy areas (old age, employment, gender equality, etc.). In the light of the recent developments in the demographic and family sectors, family policies cannot be reduced to "financial packages and family-related services within the framework of government policies. We have to take into account policy incentives by local authorities or even private, profit, non-profit, and non-governmental enterprises and organisations, etc." (Fotakis, 2000).

Table 3.4 – Full-time equivalent employment rates in various European countries by sex, 1991, 2000

Country	1991			2000		
	M	F	T	M	F	T
Belgium	70.1	38	54	74.4	46.6	60.5
Denmark	73.7	58.4	65.8	76.9	62.2	69.3
Germany	77.5	48.7	63	71.1	46.1	58.6
Greece	71.7	33.7	52.1	71.5	40	55.3
Spain	67.3	29.2	48	69	36.6	52.5
France	69.7	46	57.7	69.2	48.7	58.7
Ireland	65.4	32.1	48.9	75.8	45.2	60.6
Italy	70.8	35.5	52.9	67	36.7	51.7
Luxembourg	77	39.8	58.6	75.9	44.6	60.4
Netherlands	68.5	31.6	50	74.6	40.1	57.2
Austria	78.3 (1995)	51.2	65.8	76.2	51 (1999)	63.5
Portugal	78.7	53.5	65.5	76.6	57.1	66.6
Finland	59.1	53.8	56.5 (1995)	69.3	60.5	64.9
Sweden	72.7	60.8	66.6 (1995)	70	60.2	65.1
UK	75.7	46.1	60.4	74.4	49.7	61.7
Cyprus	79.2	47.9	47 (1999)	79.3	49.6	49
Czech Republic	77.3	58.5	67.8 (1997)	73.2	55.2	64.1
Estonia	69.7	59	64.1 (1997)	64.3	55.6	59.8
Hungary	60.1	44.5	52.1 (1996)	63.6	47.9	56
Latvia	62	52.4	57 (1998)	61.3	51.8	56.4
Lithuania	-	-	-	62.4	57.7	60
Romania	88.6	59.6	67.5 (1997)	84.6	57.3	63.8
Slovakia	65.2	51	58 (1999)	62.7	50.2	56.4
Slovenia	65.5	55.6	60.5 (1996)	66.1	56.8	61.5
EU	69.1	42.3	55.5 (1995)	71	45.3	57.9

Source:OECD, 2001.

With regard to reconciliation between work and family, we also find forces working in opposite directions in the field of family policies. While there is an increasing improvement in the rights of parents and the fundamental right of children to be reared in the best possible manner, the need to reduce public expenditure and to narrow the range of services provided for working mothers tends to lead in the opposite direction. The contradictions of this phase in European welfare regarding family policies will soon become evident, but at present women and families are experiencing increasing complications in balancing their lives.

4. Reconciling work and family: the view from inside families

Over the past twenty years, many studies have been conducted on the processes involved within the couple of sharing housework and taking care of the children. In all the countries and situations, the overall results lead us to draw the same conclusion; that given the increase in paid work for women, there should be greater family commitment by the male partner. From the point of view of equality, gender differences have certainly lessened, and men contribute more at home than they ever have, but it is equally clear that they do not do as much as they should, leaving women and mothers with the task of finding a difficult work-life balance.

The presence of persistent gender differences in the participation in the labour market, housework and childcare have inspired various theoretical approaches explaining the division between paid and unpaid work between men and women at the micro level of family organisation (for overviews, see Coltrane, 2000; Künzler, Walter, Reichart and Pfister, 2001; van Doorne-Huiskes and Willemsen, 1997; and Willemsen, Jacobs, Vossen, and Frinking, 2001). Some of these theories are gender neutral, that is they attempt to explain gender differences by means of variables and processes, which in theory would have the same effect on men and women. For instance, new home economics (Becker, 1981) and exchange theory (Cook, 1987) belong to this group. New home economics and the exchange theory[6] start from the hypothesis that individuals and families make rational choices taking into account their resources, preferences and constraints in the attempt to maximise the overall benefits they receive from their actions. Men and women are assumed to dedicate time to paid work and housework in such a way as to ensure a maximum profit, taking into account that time and money are two constraints in the decisions to be taken. Thus, if the husband earns more than the wife, the husband dedicates more time to work for the market than to household organisation.

However, this approach completely ignores the personal preferences and resources of men and women, as well as the social norms and cultural stereotypes defining male and female roles in society and the family. Naturally, the two hypotheses underlying these theories on family organisation are that housework is not only unpleasant and not very satisfying, but also not socially useful, since it is not quantifiable in the economic sense. The other hypothesis is that there are no differences between the various tasks for the family: childcare, cooking, washing, ironing, etc. are all the same and the only relevant distinction is between paid and unpaid work (Willemsen and Jacobs, 2001).

Other theories – all non-economic – hypothesise that the structures and processes operating in society have an impact on the intimate and private

---

6. The difference between the two approaches consists in the fact that new home economics considers the household as the unit of analysis, while the exchange theory focuses on the individual.

relationships of individuals, and that the experience and sensitivity of individuals cannot be separated between the private domain and the world of work (Litton Fox and McBride Murry, 2000). The theory of gender roles (Eagly, 1987) holds, for example, that behaviour is influenced by norms and values, and that there is a close relationship between behaviour and attitudes towards the roles of men and women in society. Other approaches consider the unpaid work carried out for the family and paid work for the market as a way of expressing gender identity, a sign of power and diversity in a couple relationship or an institutional context (West and Zimmerman, 1987). In this case, being a man or being a woman already constitutes an important factor in interpreting the sharing of tasks between paid and unpaid work. Gender identity is thus established by the definition of some abilities and interests as being typical of men, and others as typical of women. By behaving in a traditional manly and womanly fashion (for example, for men, not doing much housework and, for women, managing the needs of household members), men and women can fulfil gender expectations (Brines, 1993).

If we start from the hypothesis that housework partly implies the creation of correct gender relationships, we can conclude that the differences in the assignment of tasks may also express various norms regarding the responsibilities of men and women. In fact, those who study the sharing of housework from the gender point of view wonder why wives, even those who have paid work, remain wholly or partly responsible for housework. It is therefore very difficult to identify policies, other than education and training, which may affect the sharing of housework, the use of the time and the work-life balance.

Since for men and women the private family domain is the main occasion for establishing gender identities, this could explain the differences between countries, because the different living arrangements of families can depend on gender norms and stereotypes existing in a given cultural context. The social policies implemented to favour a better work-life balance could once again have different effects.

Considering a recent research study conducted by the European network on policies and the division of unpaid and paid work in seven European countries,[7] using basically the same questionnaire (Willemsen, 1997),[8] we can compare the patterns of behaviour regarding family organisation and paid work in various countries.[9] First of all, if we compare the time dedicated to paid work by men and women working in the countries studied, we find that in all

---

7. These countries were: Finland, France, Germany, Greece, Italy, the Netherlands, and Portugal.
8. The questionnaire comprised the following subjects: time use for various activities, type of employment, income, social network, household composition, use of various policy measures, use of childcare, and opinions.
9. It should be noted that the survey we are referring to is a "budget time" survey with the obvious inconvenience that is the subjective perception of time to be collected. The most precise and reliable data are those based on "time use" surveys where time diaries are compiled by respondents. Time use comparable surveys are not yet available in Europe.

the countries the men work more than the women (fifty-four hours per week on average compared to twenty-nine hours for women) (Willemsen, Jacobs, 2001).

The relationship between working hours for men and women shows that men who work, do so 1.5 times more than the women. In Germany and the Netherlands, where part-time work is widespread, the men do double the paid work done by women. Furthermore, there are extraordinary differences due to the types of household. The birth of children leads women to a drastic reduction of working hours, something that does not occur for men (Willemsen, Jacobs, 2001). Obviously, work is still a major aspect of male identity. For women, however, it does not have such an exclusive importance with respect to other factors forming their identity, resulting in the reduction, if necessary, of work times in favour of other time dedicated to family organisation.

If we examine the time dedicated to housework and childcare in families with children, we can see that women are very closely involved, and only the lone mothers reduce the time devoted to housework. The number of weekly hours they dedicate to unpaid work is, in fact, always lower than that of married and cohabiting women with children with the same employment status (Table 4.1).

Table 4.1 – Time spent per week on childcare tasks in households with at least one child

Country	Sex of respondent	Lone parent	Couple with child <7[1]	Couple with child ≥7[1]	Average of households with children
Finland	Men	--	16.5	5.2	11.9
	Women	13.2	31.7	7.2	19.0
France	Men	--	13.0	5.7	9.6
	Women	12.5	26.1	7.2	17.4
Germany	Men	--	22.5	15.6	18.7
	Women	21.9	37.8	20.8	26.5
Greece	Men	--	19.9	10.8	14.9
	Women	18.5	36.5	15.1	22.7
Italy	Men	--	19.7	7.4	12.6
	Women	--	36.0	7.0	17.0
Netherlands	Men	--	12.6	4.5	7.6
	Women	12.8	26.3	8.6	14.7
Portugal	Men	0.8	11.8	1.7	4.1
	Women	4.2	22.0	3.7	9.0
All countries	Men	6.1	17.4	7.6	11.7
	Women	15.0	33.1	12.4	20.0

Source: Willemsen and Jacobs, 2001.
1.child <7 indicates at least one child less than seven years old; child ≥7 indicates that all children (or the only child) is at least aged seven or older.

This trend among women to modify the distribution of time dedicated to paid and unpaid work according to their marital status and family stage is confirmed by studies on transition from one marital status to another, showing that for women who enter a marriage-type relationship the overall household workload increases. For men, however, forming a married or unmarried couple means a decrease in unpaid working hours for the family, work which they are in any case perfectly able to do (Sanchez et al., 1998; Gupta, 1999; and Palomba and Sabbadini, 1994). This point reconfirms the hypothesis that gender identities are established in the private domain perhaps above all through the participation in paid and unpaid work.

For women, marriage and the birth of children thus highlight the problem of gender roles in doing housework and taking care of the children. Living together under the same roof for two people of the opposite sex determines the definition of their respective gender identity through daily activities, for example in housework (West and Zimmerman, 1987; and Gupta, 1999). Therefore, although the structure of European families is developing towards the greater presence of double-income families, women must always face the task of reconciling work and family life. The presence of a lower number of children can involve a lighter burden in terms of hours dedicated to unpaid work, but the participation in paid work requires women to adopt a strategy of balance between housework and occupational tasks to be applied in any type of household.

The implications in relation to the social policies of these results are in any case difficult to determine even using reference theoretical models, as in the case of the network of the division of paid and unpaid work and policy impact, co-ordinated by the University of Tilburg (Demotrends, 2000). The main conclusions showed that family policies basically had little impact on family relationships and housework. Willemsen and Jacobs (2001) conclude by observing that, "It is still true, even in highly developed countries, that the level of education is important for workforce participation. Improving the educational level of women will help to enhance their labour-market position. It is also clear that the domain with the largest degree of inequality is the household. This poses a difficult problem for policy makers. Probably nobody likes housework. This makes it very unattractive for men to change their behaviour, and leads to feelings of dissatisfaction among women. Here, in this unglamorous domain of cleaning and cooking, lies the new challenge for egalitarian change."

5. Labour market changes

All the recent changes in the labour market are aimed at greater flexibility of work times with more employment opportunities, though with less job security. Work is therefore changing, but it is not yet clear to what extent the new processes are an advantage or create new problems for those who seek to reconcile work and family life.

"Atypical" working patterns are rapidly increasing in Europe, and involve a very large number of women. If women continue to be responsible for the strategies suited to combining work and family life, it is highly likely that part-time, casual and temporary-employment contracts or reduced working hours will apply mainly to women. This means that male and female employment will lead to unequal positions on the labour market. In other words, there is the risk that part-time work or other forms of reduced hours are actually a trap, since they destabilise the position of women on the labour market. In fact, the EU Commission has observed that "some EU member states continue to promote flexibility with little regard for the impact on gender equality" (Commission of the European Communities, 2001, p. 19).

It should also be noted that the trend towards the decrease of work time is reaching a turning point. In many European and non-European countries, there is the opposite trend, that is the increase in work time, the growth of unpaid overtime and the need to work more hours than wanted with further problems for people who work and have children (Green and McIntosh, 2000; and Schor, 1991). According to the OECD (Evans et al., 2001, p. 8), "The most striking fact about recent trends in average annual hours of work is that the long-term decline in average annual hours has slowed down in almost all OECD countries, and occasionally reversed itself. Maddison (1995) has shown that average hours of work in advanced OECD countries fell from around 3 000 hours a year in 1870 to between 1 500 and 2 000 hours a year by 1990. Apart from increases in a few countries before and during world war two, the reduction continued over the whole period. However, the situation has recently changed. For most of the 1990s, hours of work have been on an increasing trend in Hungary, Sweden and the United States, and there has been little recent change in the levels for Australia, Canada, Finland, New Zealand, Spain and the United Kingdom. The long-term trend for declining working hours continued, albeit at a generally slower pace, in France,[10] Germany, Italy, the Netherlands and Norway."

Also in the world of work, as already observed in other sectors of life, there are contradictory forces at work. Greater flexibility thus leads to an increase in the forms of work that are less stable but with reduced hours. In the overall context, however, there is an increase of the hours worked by individuals, above all full-time employees. Furthermore, the old corporate organisational models have changed or are changing rapidly; there is a focus on highly

---

10. France has introduced the legislation on the thirty-five hour week. Between September 1999 and 2000, average actual hours in France are officially estimated to have declined by 1.9%, or around thirty hours a year.

specific skills; training takes place during working life; workers must ensure a greater elasticity and ability to adapt to production changes. This involves a greater commitment (also in the psychological sense) which may become less compatible with family commitments and create problems at the time of reinsertion, for example after maternity, above all in periods of significant corporate dynamism and advancement in the field of technological innovation.

In any case, it is necessary to understand how the recent trends developed in employment influence the position of men and women on the labour market and whether the family policies created to make it easier to combine work and family are actually effective in this changing context. In general, we can group the main changes taking place in the world of work into three major categories: changes in the duration of work time (a typical example here is part-time work), changes in the control of work time (a typical example here is flexible time) and changes in the place where work takes place (a typical example here is telework).

5.1. Changes in the duration of work time

5.1.1. Reduction of work time

In many sectors of society and in the world of work, the only way to reduce the number of hours spent at paid work is to work part-time. Half of the new jobs created in Europe in the decade 1987-1997 were part-time, although the contribution of full-time jobs to the overall growth of European employment has recently become higher than that of part-time: respectively 63 % of employment growth in 1999 compared to 1990, as compared to 37 % for part-time jobs (EC, 2000). However, if we look at female employment in the EU, 47 % of the increase of employed women refers to women working part-time and over 70 % of the net additional jobs occupied by women, between 1994 and 2000, were part-time (EC, 2000) (Table 5.1).

A survey of the employment options of the future, carried out by the European foundation for the improvement of living and working conditions, shows that European workers have a growing interest in part-time work. Those who already work part-time would like a part-time job for more hours (on average twenty to twenty-five hours); some of those who work full-time would like to shift to part-time work. In this sense, if the preferences expressed by Europeans were put into practice, the overall effect on the world of work would be a reduction of the most extreme working patterns, that is those with long working hours and those with a very small number of hours (Atkinson, 1999).

Many women who do not currently work have also expressed the desire to work part-time. Their entry into the labour market would increase the active population and also the number of families with one or both partners working part-time, while the number of couples with both partners working full-time would remain more or less at current levels (Evans *et al.*, 2001).

Up to now, part-time employment contracts have been more often either temporary or casual than full-time. In fact, part-timers generally have a shorter average length of stay in the same job with respect to full-timers, and therefore less certainty in the continuity of their source of income. In many European OECD countries, few part-timers manage to keep the same job for over five years, unlike the full-timers (Evans *et al.*, 2001). Furthermore, part-timers often have fewer social benefits (or no social benefits) compared with those who have full-time and permanent employment contracts.

The possibility of voluntarily choosing to work part-time when required by the family situation, for example when there are very young children, and then to return to work full-time once the critical family stage is over, would be very important for working mothers. This transition between the two working patterns is, for the time being, basically theoretical. In case of need, the transition from full-time to part-time work and vice versa can only be implemented in Sweden and to some extent in Finland. When it becomes possible to pass from one form of work to the other, part-time work will genuinely be the best way for women to reconcile the work for the market with family responsibilities (Evans *et al.*, 2001).

The feasibility of the transition between the two working patterns is due to the existing employment policies and collective labour contracts, which protect mothers with very young children. In the Swedish case, part-time work becomes an "interlude" in a full-time career for women, while in the other cases part-time work remains a stable way of participating in the market. If the possibility of shifting from part-time back to full-time work is not guaranteed, part-time work can obviously not be considered as a choice for dealing with the family situation, when required, and can lead to gender inequality on the labour market. In fact, part-time work is always paid less than full-time work (the median hourly earning for part-timers is between 54% and 89% of that of full-timers, according to the country) and women have the lowest hourly-pay levels. These differences also persist in the same employment sector (Evans *et al.*, 2001).

Working less hours also conceals another, perhaps more subtle, problem with respect to work-family reconciliation. In fact, working less undoubtedly has an effect on the assignment of housework and family tasks. If the women are the household members who are at home for more hours, it is very unlikely to see, at least in the near future, more equal patterns of time use between men and women regarding unpaid work (domestic housework and childcare). Shorter hours might in this case very easily undermine the efforts to create a more equally shared parenthood.

Table 5.1 – Percentage of part-timers[11] in various European countries by gender, 1991-2000[12]

Country	1991			2000		
	M	F	T	M	F	T
Belgium	2.3	31	13.6	5.8	40.5	20.8
Denmark	10.8	37.8	23.3	10.2	34.1	21.3
Germany	2.5	30.2	14.1	5	37.9	19.4
Greece	2.2	7.4	3.9	2.4	7.4	4.3
Spain	1.5	11.2	4.6	2.8	16.9	8
France	3.5	23.9	12.3	5.4	31	16.9
Ireland	3.5	17.6	8.3	6.9	30.1	16.4
Italy	2.8	11.8	6	3.7	16.5	8.4
Luxembourg	-	-	-	2.0	25.0	10.5
Netherlands	15.6	60.9	33.1	19.2	70.5	41.1
Austria	4.5	26.5	14	4.1	32.2	16.3
Portugal	4.1	13	7.9	6.2	16.3	10.8
Finland	6.7	13.6	10.1	8	17	12.3
Sweden	7.3	42.8	24.2	10.6	36	22.6
UK	6.2	43.5	22.6	9.1	44.6	25
Cyprus (1999)	3.3	11.2	6.4	4.4	14.1	8.3
Czech Republic (1997)	2.9	10.3	6.1	2.2	9.5	5.4
Estonia (1997)	8.2	12.6	10.3	4.2	9.3	6.7
Hungary (1996)	2.1	4.4	3.2	2.1	5.3	3.6
Latvia (1996)	11.9	12.7	12.3	9.5	12.2	10.8
Lithuania (1998)	-	-	-	7.6	9.6	8.6
Poland (1997)	8.5	13.5	10.7	8.6	13.2	10.6
Romania (1997)	12.5	18.3	15.2	14.3	18.6	16.4
Slovakia (1999)	1.1	3.2	2.1	1	2.9	1.9
Slovenia (1996)	5.2	8.6	6.8	4.7	7.7	6.1
EU	4.1	28.3	13.9	6.2	33.3	17.7

Source: EU Employment in Europe, 2001.

5.1.2. Increase in working hours

As already observed, in many European countries an increase in the total hours worked by each worker is under way. The number of working hours is determined by a combination of regulations and collective contracts. In some countries, such as France, the influence of legislation is particularly strong; in others, such as Italy, collective bargaining through the trade unions is much more important than other aspects. If we observe the number of hours

---

11. Part-time employment refers to persons who usually work less than thirty hours per week in their main job.
12. Figures in brackets refer to the last available year if not 2000.

worked in some European countries, we can see that the trend very often shows a slight increase (Evans et al., 2001).

In some European countries, as pointed out by the OECD, unpaid over-time is very widespread. This raises the working week beyond the due limits and sometimes over fifty hours, above all where the duration of the working week is regulated by law (Evans et al., 2001). If the workers cannot exceed a certain threshold of hours by law, employers may ask employees to do more overtime, sometimes unpaid. Naturally, this is only a trend for now which could, however, become stronger in the near future. The negative effects of these trends with regard to compatibility between work and family are easy to foresee and hard to overcome through individual and family decisions. The employers will, in fact, tend to reward and deem to be efficient and reliable those workers who follow corporate-productivity policy and show their commitment at the cost of limiting their private life. The time spent at work thus becomes a gender-equity issue, since, as we know, women have to deal with family and childcare commitments.

5.2. Changes in the control of work time

The 1980s and 1990s have been defined as the years of the introduction of flexible work time. In the light of market deregulation, globalisation and the need to adapt production processes to a changing society, the standard working week based on forty hours for five days has undergone profound changes (Breedveld, 2001; and Boulin and Muckenberger, 1999). The flexibility of work time is often considered as a possibility offered to workers to exercise greater control over their own time, and to have more freedom to choose working hours better suited to the needs of life. Therefore, flexibility is interpreted as a general reduction of the constraints imposed on the work-life balance of workers.

If we examine the Eurostat labour force survey data, we can see that flexible work time actually means a different way of distributing work during the day (working in shifts, in which workers follow each other in the same job, in the evening and night) and during the week (working on Saturday and Sunday). Often flexi-time is associated with part-time work. A total of 13% of European employees work in shifts; 37% work evenings (at least sometimes), 15% work nights; a rather large percentage, 51%, work on Saturdays (also sometimes); and 28% work on Sundays. Of all European countries, flexi-work is especially common in the UK; Ireland and Greece. Belgium, Germany, France, Luxembourg, Austria, the Netherlands and Italy generally score below EU averages (Table 5.2).

Table 5.2 – Percentage of those employed with shift-work, evening-work, night-work, work on Saturday, work on Sunday in EU countries in 1997, and changes from 1993-1997

Country	1997[a]						1993-1997[b]				
	Shifts	Evening	Night	Saturday	Sunday	Index	Shifts	Evening	Night	Saturday	Sunday
Austria	21	30	18	47	27	97	na	na	na	na	na
Belgium	16	34	14	40	25	88	0.2	-0.2	-0.4	0.1	1.2
Denmark	9	39	15	47	37	107	-0.5	-1.1	-1.6	-2.6	0.1
Finland	23	50	20	40	29	113	na	na	na	na	na
France	8	34	15	53	29	100	0.7	1	0.3	0.2	1.8
Germany	12	32	13	41	23	84	0.4	4	-1	3.6	2
Greece	11	65	14	64	33	128	0.5	2.5	0.2	0.8	0
Ireland	14	35	21	60	36	120	0.2	-3	-1.5	-0.7	-0.6
Italy	18	29	13	62	22	91	-0.2	1.5	0.8	-0.8	0.7
Luxembourg	12	27	13	42	23	81	-5.1	0.6	-0.9	2.6	0.7
Netherlands	8	27	11	42	25	79	0.2	1.3	0.4	2.5	2.3
Portugal	7	1	1	38	16		-0.3	0.3	-0.1	4.5	2.3
Spain	7	-	11	42	19	104	1.0	-	1.4	-0.7	1.3
Sweden	27	42	14	41	36	151	na	na	na	na	na
UK	18	57	24	65	45		1.4	1.8	-0.4	1.9	2.4
EU average[c]	13	37	15	51	28	100	0.5	2	0	1.4	1.8

a. In all cases: those working "sometimes" or "often/regularly".
b. Increase/decrease 1997 percentage from 1993 percentage.
c. 1997 over all countries, difference 1997-1993 only over countries with surveys in 1993 and 1997.
Source: Eurostat/Labour force surveys.

Flexi-time working practices therefore require an increase of work time during the weekend and the evening, especially in services-related jobs involving an overwhelming percentage of women. It is very difficult to understand without relevant information, even on a sample basis, and without specific impact studies, whether flexible work actually gives workers greater control of their time. Many researchers have challenged the idea that these forms of work provide this opportunity (Elchardus, 1991; and Breedveld, 1998) and it seems highly likely that workers have very limited scope for choosing which form of work-time organisation is best suited to their own rhythms.

Furthermore, requests for more flexible work time often occur on an individual basis and do not regard collective labour contracts, thus requiring a negotiation ability that not all workers have. This may lead to favouritism and unfairness. It can put women in a difficult situation, since they need to combine family and work commitments and often have less bargaining power. Breedveld, in fact, concludes his analysis on the introduction of flexi-time in Europe by stating (Breedveld, 2001, p. 9): "We did not find support for the 'flexibility equals control' thesis. In virtually every European country, those in higher positions experience more control over their working time than those in lower positions. The same holds true for men and women, with men reporting more control than women. And though this in no way implies that people working evenings, nights and weekends are deprived of the possibility to enjoy their hobbies or to spend time with their loved ones, it does show that there exist in Europe clear inequalities in the capacities to profit from new, more varied and diverging time structures."

The increase in flexibility in the world of work must therefore advance with the principles of social justice and gender equality if we really want the new working patterns and work-time organisation to also produce family-friendly effects.

5.3. Changes in the workplace

The most recent change in the world of work is the possibility of working while staying at home. Telework is by definition the type of activity in which workers do their work staying at home either on a regular basis (home-based telework) or alternating periods of work at home and periods of work in the central offices (alternating telework form). There are also other forms of telework in which the work conducted outside the offices is above all occasional. Working at home provides the possibility of combining work and family commitments in the way best suited to people's needs. Obviously, not all work can be done in this way, but the computerisation of many production processes is certainly leading to an increase in this form of work.

Data on the diffusion of telework in the enterprises of ten countries (Telework data report, 2000) show that this concerns about 30% of the employees. The Scandinavian countries and the United Kingdom are leading in this field. The Netherlands, Ireland and France form the middle field. Given the proportion of establishments that practise telework only Spain and Italy lag behind Germany (Table 5.3).

Table 5.3 – Establishments practising home-based telework in Europe 1999 (in % of all establishments)

Country	Alternating telework	Home-based telework
Denmark	24.85	26.85
Finland	18.58	22.40
France	6.42	8.33
Germany	12.16	13.30
Ireland	10.11	13.53
Italy	2.94	4.66
Netherlands	16.00	18.67
Spain	7.47	7.83
Sweden	20.41	22.35
UK	20.57	24.47

Source: Telework data report, 2000.

It would be very useful to have studies conducted on the impact of telework on household organisation, since without this information we can only advance hypotheses and assumptions. If women are involved in telework, the gender inequalities in dealing with housework and childrearing, already observed previously, cannot but increase. Furthermore, the mechanism of occupational segregation, in which women are always at the lowest rungs of the hierarchical ladder, could become even more discriminatory in the presence of "virtual" workers who do not participate, in any way, in corporate life. The time and physical presence at the workplace are, in fact, key aspects in the equality of treatment and for the acknowledgement of abilities.

6. Concluding remarks

When we analyse the problems of reconciling work and family, we either tend to stress the similarities between countries, thus highlighting any "convergence" points, or to look at the differences, thus highlighting a historical and cultural approach. In any case, as we have seen in this report, similarities and differences coexist, and whatever the point of view chosen it is very difficult to find a country that could be considered as a model for best practices.

In many respects, the Scandinavian countries are a positive example in the general European context. We should recall, however, that economic development and the integration of women into the labour market could follow different pathways, if the historical and cultural context of the countries fails to take into account the need to find a fair "gender compromise." The focus in the Scandinavian countries on respecting the principles of equality between men and women and the symmetry of gender roles in the private family domain have been achieved by women through their strong commitment in political life. If this is the factor that has produced the profound change of mentality in northern Europe regarding equity and equal opportunities for men and women, this means that it is a model which it is impossible to export to other countries with a different background (Daune-Richard, 1995).

Conditions of families vary widely across Europe, depending on social, cultural, and economic factors. These are distinctive from country to country and from region to region. However, all countries attach a fundamental importance to the family as being "the natural environment for the growth and well-being of all its members and particularly children" (European ministers responsible for family affairs, 1999). In order to enable everything discussed above to become a reality, certain conditions need to be fulfilled. These include, firstly, the provision of freedom of choice to a couple in its decision to have a child; secondly, there should be a clear societal commitment to facilitate responsible and enjoyable parenthood, and thirdly, help and support should be provided to families when needed.

6.1. Freedom of choice and work-life balance

In European countries, changes in social, cultural, demographic and economic structures over the last twenty years have radically altered the context in which parents bring up children. One result of these changes is the high and continuously rising level of education of young women in all European countries combined with their wish for more autonomous life-choices.

European women are having children when they are older. The period when they are bringing up their children thus coincides with the time when they should be starting to find a foothold on the occupational ladder and in the case of the most highly skilled, building a career. The constraints are particularly severe during the period when the children are not independent. Despite the official statements about the need to guarantee respect for freedom of choice of families, couples and individuals, to be realised within the legal framework of national social protection systems (Council of Europe, 1998), this "choice" is still largely a pipedream for many Europeans. Most women would like to have a choice of whether to continue working after their child is born, but in many families two incomes are necessary to attain a decent standard of living. Mothers may ask for a reduction in working time at specific stages of their life cycle to improve the balance between working life and personal or family life, but they often are not aware of the medium and long-term consequences of their choices in terms of career progression and pension levels.

The freedom to choose among alternative options may be considered a fundamental human right from which all other human rights derive. However, the freedom to choose is not absolute, for it may conflict with other rights and freedoms; the choice must be informed, which requires information that is accessible, objective, comprehensive and personalised, to let people choose being conscious of potential disadvantages and side effects of their decision; and it is also contingent upon the state's fulfilment of certain social and economic entitlements that make genuine choice possible. Whatever kind of society we live in, individual freedom of choice can only exist under certain conditions. Keeping things simple and having in mind the reconciliation between work and family, we may conclude that the following three conditions need to be met: a) there must be choices that can be made by parents and mothers in particular; b) the law must protect and uphold the individual's freedom to choose; c) the consequences of the choices cannot be faced only by a specific group inside the society (such as women, for example).

As we have seen, the "right to choose" is not completely guaranteed in the everyday life of families in all European countries, because the possibility of mothers and parents to make their choices is largely dependent on the economic conditions of the families themselves; the other two points mentioned above have to do with the concept of equal opportunities, that is the fundamental basis for the freedom of choice but it should not be absorbed or confused by the latter.

6.2. Work v. family: still an undeniable dichotomy

Female job and career opportunities and their relation with family matters are a complex reality. "Internal" factors depending on the organisation, functioning, and structure of the labour market must be part of that reality. These are in turn interdependent upon the "external" factors that pertain to society at large for example existing gender roles inside and outside the family, the changing status of women in education and the labour market, and the political framework for equal opportunities. This report did not attempt to discuss whether the causalities are specific to sectors of the labour market or country specific, or whether they are part of a wider problem in society as a whole. What it did attempt to do was to present an overview of the presence and participation of women in the labour market, and to show persistent gaps in terms of equal opportunities and gender equity in European countries, which may negatively affect the working life of women and the possibilities to reconcile work and family.

In fact, in the countries where a link between the women's movement and political power has neither been developed nor sought, the request for equal opportunities between the men and women has been confined to the production sector. This has resulted – though with differences between the various countries – in an increase in the female presence on the market, without developing and regulating a work-life balance suited to the new family needs.

The idea of having to reconcile work and family or to find a work-life balance implies a dichotomy between two parts of life which fail to communicate properly, and require people somehow to divide their time between the two. This divide, as we have seen, does not take place in a simple way, since choosing commitment to one of the two sectors of life implies a certain amount of sacrifice of the other. From the demographic point of view, this "sacrifice" can lead to a fall in fertility; from the family point of view, it produces an unbalanced shift of childcare and housework towards women; from the working point of view, it may mean a reduction of career opportunities for those who choose to reduce work time, thus dedicating much more time to the family. The need to reconcile work and family is thus inevitably marked by the gender divide.

Family-friendly policies alone are not sufficient to solve the problem of the reconciliation between private family life and work. These measures do not, in fact, introduce any systematic and substantial change into the culture and organisation of the world of work. Consequently, people, and above all women who use existing possibilities to find a better balance between work and family, basically by reducing work time or by breaks in working life (maternity and parental leaves, sick-child leave, part-time, flexi-time, etc.), end up by suffering a negative impact in economic terms or with an overload of housework due to their choices.

6.3. Changing the work practices

The core of the solution is not, therefore, somehow to find a compromise between work and family, leaving the two parts separate or in conflict, but to accept the principle that the objectives and priorities of individuals can be different, and that men and women have the right to freely experience and live these two parts of their life, combining them and not necessarily seeking a difficult balance.

This integration has nothing to do with the rights to take care of children, who, as weaker groups of the population, are protected in the European countries by highly advanced Community and national legislation, but rather with the overcoming of the profound separation still characterising the world of work and the family and with the "underlying assumptions about men's and women's roles in family, community, and paid work, assumptions that shape our workplaces as they shape all our social institutions" (Rapaport et al., 2002). The necessary changes cannot be just political and on the macro-economic level, but must be focused on working to change the "culture of work".

We must go to a lower level of changes in the existing legislative context or of the market rules, since integration between private life and work must be faced and solved at the level of the individual company or job context. The organisations providing employment must become more family-friendly, more sensitive and open to those who want to work and continue to "lead their own life". As long as there is a widespread conviction in the workplace that there must be a hierarchy in the values and behaviour of the employees based on the view that work is more important than any other aspect of peoples' lives, the career and employment opportunities for those who make different choices or who are forced to find a compromise between work commitments and personal life will necessarily be limited.

The literature describes some experiments at the company level[13] confirming how it is possible to follow this way, showing employers that the efficiency of employees is not necessarily linked to their prolonged physical presence at the workplace (Perrons, 1999; and Rapaport et al., 2002).

We must always keep in mind that all the transformations described in this report regarding the world of work have a substantially economic basis, and work-family reconciliation is only applicable on a secondary basis. This is why it is impossible to refer to new working patterns (part-time, flexi-time, tele-work) as a panacea to cure Europe's social problems, to achieve an adequate work-life balance and to ensure workers better working conditions. We can find positive examples, at the national level or in individual enterprises, where the introduction of a mixture of these options (with the introduction of flexibility and computerisation of production processes) has actually contributed to better achieving the reconciliation between company-level efficiency and better living arrangements for the workers. We note, for example, the introduction in Austria of the "Family and employment audit" which assists enterprises in implementing family-friendly, but nevertheless economically efficient company policies. The audit grants state awards to companies with family-friendly policies (Austrian national report, 1999). However, these are always experiments which cannot be repeated elsewhere without more or less extensive adaptations.

---

13. Among the best known, we can recall Xerox Corporation.

For many parents, the task of raising children in modern societies like those in Europe, which stress individual adaptation to rapid changes, and which seek to be internationally oriented and economically competitive, is becoming increasingly difficult. While in Europe work in the future will be more flexible – in the broadest sense of the term – this will probably attract more women onto the market, but will only create the necessary pre-conditions to make work more compatible with family needs, and further guarantees and rules should be introduced so that these changes do not become in the long term an economic trap for the families and parents taking advantage of them.

References

Allan, G., Hawker S., G. Crow. 2001. "Family diversity and change in Britain and western Europe", *Journal of Family Issues,* 22 (7):pp. 819-837.

Austrian national report. 1999. UN The Hague forum, 8-12 February.

Baylin, L. 1993. *Breaking the mould: women, men and time in the new corporate world,* New York: Free Press.

Bailey, L. 2000. "Bridging home and work in the transition to motherhood", *European journal of women's studies,* pp. 53-70.

Becker, G. S. (1981/1991). *A treatise on the family.* Cambridge: Harvard University Press.

Bernhart, E.M. 1993. "Fertility and employment." *European sociological review,* 9: pp. 25-42.

Bradshaw, J., Corden A., Holmes H., Hutton S., Kennedy S., Kilkey M., J. Neale. 1996. *Why and how do lone parents work outside the home? A comparison of twenty countries,* York: Joseph Rowntree foundation-European Commission.

Boulin, Jean-Y., U. Muckenberger. 1999. *Times in the city and the quality of life.* Dublin: European foundation for working and living conditions.

Breedveld, K. 1998. "The double myth of flexibilization." *Time and Society* 7(1): pp. 129-144.

Breedveld, K. 2001. "Flexibility and control over working time: a European perspective", paper presented at 8th international symposium on working time, Diemen, The Netherlands, 14-16 March.

Brines, J. 1993. "The exchange value of housework." *Rationality and society.* 5: pp. 302-340.

Bruning, G., J. Plantenga. 1999. Parental leave and equal opportunities: experiences in eight European countries, *Journal of European social policy,* 9(3): pp. 195-209.

Carnoy, N. 1999. "The family, flexible work and social cohesion at risk." *International labour review.* 138 (4): pp. 411-29.

Council of Europe. 1998. Recommendation No. R (98) 9 of the Committee of Ministers to member states on dependence, adopted by the Committee of Ministers at the 641st meeting of the Ministers' Deputies, 18 September.

Colin, C. 1995. "L'éventail des salaires par profession" – *Insee Première* n°366.

Coltrane, S. 2000. "Research on household labor: Modeling and measuring the social embeddedness of routine family work." *Journal of marriage and the family,* 62: pp. 1208-1233.

Cook, K. S., (ed.). 1987. *Social exchange theory.* Newbury Park: Sage Publications.

Daune-Richard, A.M. 1995. "Women's employment and different societal effects in France, Sweden, and the UK". *International journal of sociology.* 25 (2): pp.39-65.

Demotrends. 2000. *Division of paid and unpaid work,* 1, IRP:Rome.

Drew, E., Emerek R., E. Mahon, (eds). 1998. *Women, work and family in Europe* London: Routledge.

Eagly, A. H. 1987. *Sex differences in social behavior: A social role interpretation.* Hillsdale, NJ: Erlbaum.

Elchardus, M. 1991. "Flexible men and women. The changing temporal organisation of work and culture: an empirical analysis". *Social science information* 30(4): pp. 701-725.

European Commission. 2001. *Annual report on equal opportunities for women and men in the European Union 2000,* COM (2001) 179.

European Commission. *Employment in Europe 2000,* Internet site.

European Commission. 1998. *Parental leave in European Union countries. New ways to work,* Brussels: European Network "family and work" and new ways to work survey.

Evans, M.J., Douglas C.L., M. Pascal. 2001. "Trends in working hours in OECD countries", OECD *Occasional Papers,* 45, Paris.

Fernandez-Cordon, J.A. 1997. "Youth residential independence and autonomy: a comparative study". *Journal of family issues,* XVIII, 6.

Fotakis, C. 2000. "Presentation of social report", paper presented at European observatory on family matters; Annual seminar: *Low fertility, families and public policies,* Seville (Spain), 15–16 September.

Gauthier, A. 2000. "Public policies affecting fertility in Europe: a survey of the fifteen member states", paper presented at European observatory on family matters; Annual seminar: *Low fertility, families and public policies,* Seville (Spain), 15–16 September.

Goldberg Shaffner, G., 2001.Three stages of welfare capitalism, in Goldberg Shaffner G., M.G. Rosenthaleds, *Diminishing welfare,* London: Auburn House.

Goldberg Shaffner, G., M.G. Rosenthal, (eds).2001, *Diminishing welfare,* London: Auburn House.

Green, F., S. McIntosh. 2000. "Working on the chain gang? An examination of rising effort levels in Europe in the 1990s", London School of Economics and Political Science, Centre for economic performance, *Discussion paper,* No. 465.

Gupta, S. 1999. "The effects of transition in marital status on men's perform-ance of housework", *Journal of marriage and the family,* 61: pp. 700-711.

Goode, W.J. 200. *World changes in divorce patterns,* New Haven: Yale Uni-versity Press.

Hardy S., N. Adnett. 2001. *The parental leave directive: towards a `family-friendly' social Europe?* Paper 2001.09, Division of economics, Staffordshire University business school.

Hochschild, A. 1989. *The second shift: working parents and the revolution at home,* New York: Viking.

Holden, K., P. Smock. 1991. "The economic cost of marital dissolution: why do women bear a disproportionate cost?" *Annual review of sociology* 17: pp. 51-78.

Hughes, R. jr, J.D. Hans. 2001. "Computers, the Internet and families" *Journal of Family Issues,* 22 (6): pp. 776-791.

Künzler, J., Walter, W., Reichart, E., and G. Pfister. 2001. *Gender division of labour in unified Germany.* WORC Report 01.04.07,Tilburg University: Work and organisation research centre.

Lachs Ginsgurg, H., M.G. Rosenthal. 2001. "Sweden: temporary detour or new directions?", in Goldberg Shaffner G., M.G. Rosenthal (eds), *Diminishing welfare,* London: Auburn House. pp. 103-147.

Lewis, J. 2001. "Social insurance and future work", in *Labour law and social insurance in the new economy: a debate on the Supiot report',* London School of Economics and Political Science, Centre for economic performance, Discussion paper No. 500.

Litton Fox, G., V. Mc Bride Murry. 2000. "Gender and families: feminist per-spectives and family research" *Journal of marriage and the family,* 62: pp. 1160-1172.

Maddison, A. 1995. *Monitoring the world economy,* pp. 1820-1992, Paris: OECD.

Menniti, A., M. Misiti. 2000. "Italian staying at home children", paper presented at Workshop *Leaving home - a European focus,* Max Planck Institute for demographic research, Rostock, 6-8 September.

Moss, P., F. Deven. 2000. *Parental leave: progress or pitfall?,* Brussels: NIDI-CBGS Publications.

National Board of Health and Welfare-NBHW. 1997. *Social and caring services in Sweden,* Linköpings: Linköpings Trychery AB.

Nebenführ, E. 1998. "Determinants of preferences regarding work and family", in Palomba R., H. Moors (eds), *Population, family and welfare,* vol. 2, pp. 143-162, Oxford: Clarendon University Press.

O' Reilly, J. 1996. "Theoretical considerations in cross-national employment research." *Sociological research online,* vol. 1, no. 1.

OECD. 1994. The OECD jobs study, OECD, Paris.

OECD. 2001. "Balancing work and family life: Helping parents into paid employment", Chapter 4 of *Employment outlook,* June 2001, OECD: Paris.

Orloff, A.S. 1993. "Gender and social rights of citizenship", *American sociological review,* 58 (3): pp. 303-328.

Palomba, R., L.L. Sabbadini. 1994. *Different times,* Rome: Istat-Commissione Nazionale Pari Opportunit.

Perrons, D. 1999. "Flexible working patterns and equal opportunities in the EU" *The European journal of women's studies,* 6: pp. 391-418.

Pierson, P. 1994. *Dismantling the welfare state? Reagan, Thatcher and the politics of retrenchment,* Cambridge: Cambridge University Press.

Pierson, P. 1996. "The new politics of the welfare state". *World politics,* 48: pp. 143-179.

Prinz, C. 1995. *Cohabiting, married and single.* Averbury: Aldershot.

Rapaport, R., R.N. Rapaport, 1971. *Dual-career families,* Harmondsworth: Penguin.

Sanchez, L., Manning W.D. P.J. Smock. 1998. "Union transition among cohabiters." *Social science research,* 27: pp. 280-304.

Schor, J. 1991. *The overworked American,* New York: Basic Books.

Taskinen, S. 2000. "Alternative child-care policies and fertility", paper presented at European observatory on family matters; Annual seminar: *Low fertility, families and public policies,* Seville (Spain), 15–16 September.

Van Doorne-Huiskes, A., T. M. Willemsen. 1997. Time allocation as a major issue. In K. Tijdens, A. van Doorne-Huiskes and T. M. Willemsen (eds), *Time allocation and gender. The relationship between paid labour and household work,* 213-229. Tilburg: Tilburg University Press.

West, C., D.H. Zimmerman. 1987."Doing gender" *Gender and society,* 1: pp. 125-151.

Willemsen, T. M. 1997. *European network on policies and the division of unpaid and paid work: survey questionnaire.* WORC Paper 97.06.003/ 6.Tilburg: Tilburg University, Work and organisation research centre.

Willemsen, T. M., M. J. G. Jacobs. 2001. "Looking for new patterns of work and care: an international overview", Paper presented at the symposium *New patterns of family relations,* Tilburg, 29 June.

Willemsen, T. M., Jacobs, M. J. G., Vossen, A., G. A. B. Frinking. 2001. "An impact assessment of policy measures to influence the gender division of work." *Evaluation,* 7: pp. 369-386.

Internet sites related to the topic

www.europa.int: European Commission site. It is possible to download Euro-barometers surveys.

http://www.ilo.org: The International Labour Organization is the UN spe-cialized agency which seeks the promotion of social justice and internation-ally recognized human and labour rights.

http://www.ipu.org/: IPU is the international organisation of parliaments of sovereign states. The union is the focal point for world-wide parliamentary dialogue and its headquarters are in Geneva (Switzerland).

http://www.leeds.ac.uk: Centre for the study of law in Europe.

http://www.nsd.uib.no/cessda/index.htm: CESSDA provides a multilingual, integrated data catalogue allowing users to search up to eleven social science data catalogues located all over the world, including catalogues in Israel, Australia, the US, and Europe. In addition, the site supplies three clickable international maps that link users to the sites of thirty-two other data archives.

http://www.oecd.org/: descriptions of OECD statistics available in printed publications, discs, and tapes.

http://www.policylibrary.com/: the aim of the policy library is to place policy research and analysis in the public domain. The library has two parts: the first a database of online policy and research papers drawn from individual research institutions, think tanks and government departments; the second, in some policy areas, an attempt to place papers in context through subjective literature reviews. The focus is initially on the UK but plans are to progressively cover institutions in the English-speaking world.

http://www.reformmonitor.org/: this website gives a wide range of selected information on social policies (health care, pensions provision, family policy, state welfare), labour market policy and industrial relations in fifteen OECD countries: Australia, Austria, Canada, Denmark, Finland, France, Germany, Italy, Japan, the Netherlands, Spain, Sweden, Switzerland, United Kingdom and the United States of America. It is part of the "International reform monitor" project by the Bertelsmann Foundation.

http://www.un.org/womenwatch/: the United Nations bodies that deal with the advancement and empowerment of women.

http://www.unece.org/: UN Economic Commission for Europe site.

http://unicc.org/: the International computing centre (ICC) was established in Geneva in 1971 as a co-operative set up, providing a wide range of computing and communication services, on a cost recovery basis, to its users world-wide.

http://www.unifem.undp.org/: the UN site for women's empowerment and gender equality.

http://www.unfpa.org/: this is the site of the UN population fund and it is possible to find documents and reports on the topics in various languages plus links to suggested topics.

http://www.workliferesearch.org/: the Work-life Research Centre aims to increase understanding about the relationships between employment, care, family and community; to stimulate active dialogue and exchange of experience and perspectives between the many different parties with an interest in these relationships; and to support the development of policy and practice in workplace, community and society to increase organisational effectiveness, quality of life and equality of opportunity.

http://www.un.org/popin/: POPIN is a decentralised community of population institutions organised into regional and national networks in Africa, Asia and the Pacific, Latin America and the Caribbean, Europe and northern America. POPIN's website includes statistical tables, software, official documentation of the International conference on population and development.

http://www.un.org/womenwatch/index.html: the United Nations Internet gateway on the advancement and empowerment of women. Includes statistical data (that is population, households and families, health, education, employment) by country, national and regional plans of action, and national contacts.

http://www.un.org/Depts/unsd/gs_natstat.htm: from the United Nations statistics office links to the statistical agencies in most countries, and comparisons of countries against United Nations social and economic indicators.

http://www.worldbank.org: World Bank site with a special focus on poverty and development.

II. Older workers in the labour market and retirement policies

Irena E. Kotowska

1. Introduction

The clear trend towards lower labour force participation of persons aged 55 and more has been observed in European countries with developed market economies over many years. During the last decade similar changes took place in the transition countries of central and eastern Europe. The population ageing as well as the labour force ageing has accompanied the decline in the economic activity of older workers. Together with relatively high and persistent unemployment and the expected decrease in the size of the labour force, this phenomenon is a cause for serious concern about the financial viability of public pension systems. These are predominantly funded on a pay-as-you-go (PAYG) basis, so the rising imbalance between the number of contributors to these systems and their beneficiaries will have significant implications for funding arrangements. The different initiatives, in place in various countries, which seek to stimulate the labour force participation of older workers illustrate the importance attached by governments to reversing the trend towards earlier retirement.

Usually challenges faced by pension systems are considered in terms of the ageing of the population and labour force, labour market related factors, and changes in family structures. The ageing of the population and labour force is mostly exposed in public perception of issues related to pension systems, however labour market developments seem to become increasingly relevant. Certainly the change in family structures receives much less attention.

The labour market has become highly dynamic and unstable. Technological progress provokes rapid and unstable changes in the demand for labour. Quantity mismatch between labour supply and labour demand is increasingly replaced by quality mismatch. Labour supply adjustments to these demand-oriented changes result, among other things, in high and persistent unemployment and changing work patterns, that is more temporary jobs, and part-time work, etc. Moreover, on average employment tenure is becoming more precarious. Since most old-age pensions are based on contributory schemes with eligibility requirements, and the level of payment is linked to a person's work record and salary, changes in labour force experiences can negatively affect the accumulation of future pension rights.

Among changes in family arrangements, those related to family formation and dissolution seem to affect a provision of pension-based incomes for dependent spouses. Despite growing female participation in the labour market, a significant group of women is still not in paid work and many pension systems provide some form of income coverage for dependent spouses of the employed. The increasing frequency of cohabitation and divorces poses some challenges for the pension rights of those women who were not active in the labour market. Also, the declining number of children, on one hand, and the difficulties experienced by young labour market entrants, on the other, reduce the possibilities of children providing financial assistance to their parents if they are in need. Regulations on old-age pensions should reflect these socio-economic developments as well.

The clearly visible declining labour force participation of older workers is mainly due to the population's increased living standards, and the incentives embedded in social security systems. However, under the increasing dynamics of the labour market, inadequate flexibility of the old labour force might be considered as a factor of increasing relevance. That flexibility could be discussed in terms of desired changes in work patterns which lead to more flexible and diversified work contracts (temporary work, part-time work, the fragmentation of work), steadily upgrading skills to cope with new technologies, and spatial mobility. Older workers may experience some difficulties in meeting these requirements. It is also noteworthy that technological pressure may increasingly affect the withdrawal of older workers from the labour market.

The report focuses on the changes in economic activity of older workers and their determinants related to the labour market and institutional factors. Mostly supply effects are considered (the size and age composition of the labour force, old-age pensions and other non-employment related schemes), however, demand related factors (structure of the economy, high and persistent unemployment, technological progress) are also referred to.

The report starts with a brief overview of different changes in the working-age population (15-64 years), which constitutes the potential labour force. Its size and age composition (15-24, 25-54, 55-64 age groups) are carefully studied across selected countries. The ageing of the labour force deserves special attention. The synthetic description, based on Council of Europe data, covers the years 1990-2000. An evaluation of future trends refers to the UN population projections of 2000 (medium variant for the years 2000-2050).[14] The descriptive analysis aims to present general trends and country differences as regards changes in the labour force and acceleration in the ageing of the labour force.

---

14. That medium variant has also been used to study future ageing in Europe by Maškov (2002).

Then there is an examination of trends towards lower labour force participation of persons aged 55 and more. This has been observed in European countries with developed market economies for many years now. During the last decade similar changes took place in the transition countries of central and eastern Europe. In seeking to explain these trends, some results of empirical studies in that field are presented. Retirement policies can be discussed in terms of existing retirement income arrangements, other non-employment benefit systems and reforms of pension systems. The latter two have both been undertaken recently, and have sought to adapt the pension system to the challenges raised by demographic, economic and social developments. The report focuses on existing public defined-benefit pension systems with special attention focused on work disincentives. During a short discussion on pension system reforms, measures oriented at promoting economic activity among older workers will receive special consideration.

The country coverage includes European Union (EU) members (except for Luxembourg), Norway, Switzerland and ten transition countries (including some central European countries and the Baltic states). That particular selection of transition countries has resulted from labour market data availability. Despite steadily improved labour market statistics in post-socialist countries, including the implementation of labour force surveys, there are still some obstacles to finding comparable data for all European countries. Therefore, the scope of data on demographic trends might be slightly different from that of data on labour market participation. In the report the term "western countries" is used for the first group of countries and "transition countries" for the second one.

It was also not possible to apply the same time perspective on changes in the labour force participation of persons aged 55 and over for both groups of countries: "western" countries and transition countries. Long-term decline in economic activity is only pertinent to western countries. Moreover, that topic has recently been thoroughly studied. For this reason, only selected findings have been presented here.

For transition countries, only recent data from the last decade can be referred to, this is International Labour Organization (ILO), Eurostat and Organisation for Economic Co-operation and Development (OECD) data. The main labour market issue is a decline in overall economic activity, and unemployment. The declining labour participation of older workers is not perceived as a primary issue. However, the rapidly shrinking contribution base for the social security system, coupled with rising expenditure, on one hand, and projected rapid increase of the elderly population accompanied by a decline in the labour force, on the other, has drawn attention to pension systems. The number of studies on challenges faced by pension systems and the need for fundamental reforms has been increased recently. The report refers predominantly to studies carried out by international agencies under specially focused projects. These are mainly research reports by the World Bank, the ILO and the OECD.

2. Demographics of the labour market

The slowing population growth in Europe and the ageing of the European population have been discussed intensively for at least two decades now. The shrinking labour force and the increasing labour force decline have become topics for debate relatively recently. Changes in the size and age structure of the working-age population are accompanied by a decline in the labour market participation of significant population groups. Moreover, despite regional differences in the pace of change, the phenomenon itself is becoming widespread. Therefore, the economic and social consequences of the labour force decline and ageing, along with the ageing population, are topics which are broadly debated and studied by demographers and economists alike.

2.1. Situation at the turn of the century

The growth of the working-age population in western countries slowed down in the second half of the 1990s. In transition countries that population has continuously been growing. As a result, in 2001 the share of the working-age population was slightly lower in the first group than in the second group of countries (67% v. 69%) (see Table 1 in the appendix).

All countries under consideration are experiencing an increase in the share both of people older than 65 and of those aged 55-64, in other words population and labour force ageing. Regional differences in population ageing are discussed in depth by Maškov (2002). Differences due to previous changes in fertility and mortality, and migration, especially if they occurred during the second demographic transition, have contributed to a visible regional distinction between transition countries and the developed market economies in terms of ageing advancement: in the former the share of the elderly ranges from 10%-15 %, while in the majority of the latter that share varies between 15%-18%.

Furthermore, the ageing of the working-age population is diversified across countries. The potential labour force in transition countries is visibly younger: the share of 15-24 year old populations ranges from 21% to 25%, while in western countries it does not exceed 21% (except for Ireland). Germany, with the lowest share of young people, is followed by Italy. However, the share of people aged 55-64 accounts for 13%-20% of the working-age population in western countries (Germany is again the leader followed by Sweden). In transition countries the highest value at nearly 18%, is found in Latvia, and the lowest (12%), in Poland (see Table 1 in the appendix).

Figure 1 – The percentage of persons aged 55-64 in the working-age population, 2001

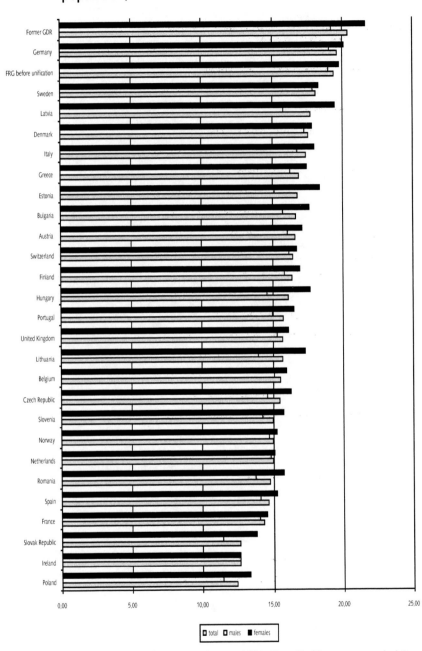

Source: Recent demographic developments in Europe, 2001, Council of Europe, own calculations.

Due to differences in life expectancy according to gender, the male working-age population is not ageing as fast as the female labour force. Again, the unfavourable changes in mortality in central and eastern Europe which started in the second half of the 1960s, especially with respect to males, make these gender differences more visible for the transition countries, and in particular for the Baltic states (see Table 1a and Table 1b in the appendix, and Figure 1). In western countries the percentage of older males and females are 16.7% and 16.9% respectively, while in transition countries these values are 13.3% and 15.5%.

The proportion between the working-age population and those in the non-working-age group reflects the pressure put upon the potential labour force. Because of declining fertility, persons aged up to 14 contribute less and less to that pressure. However, the elderly are increasingly exerting more pressure on the potential labour force. Furthermore, regional differences in the rise in the number of elderly persons (aged 65 and over), as well as in the working-age population, mean that the elderly dependency ratio is strongly diversified across regions and countries.

There are nearly 20 elderly persons per 100 working-age people in transition countries, as compared with 24 elderly persons for western countries. Italy, Sweden, Belgium and Greece are at the top of the list (26-27 persons) while the Netherlands and Ireland are at the bottom (17 and 20 persons – see Figure 2). Generally, southern and north-western parts of Europe have the highest values of the elderly dependency ratio. In transition countries, the most significant disparity between the working-age population and the elderly is found in Bulgaria (24 persons), Estonia and Latvia (nearly 23 persons) while the lowest dependency ratio can be observed in the Slovak Republic and Poland (17 and 18 persons respectively).

Gender differences in the elderly dependency ratios are markedly higher than those observed in the labour force ageing rate. The values for males are nearly 10 persons lower than for females in western countries and 9 persons lower in transition countries. These gender differences in effective ratios (persons aged 65 and more compared to the active population aged 15-64) are most probably so significant due to differences in the labour force participation of males and females.

Among the various demographic developments observed in the 1990s, those related to mortality seem to be relevant for both population and labour force ageing as assessed at the turn of the twentieth century. They can be demonstrated by life expectancy at age 45 and 65 shifts (e(45) and e(65)).

Furthermore, changes in life expectancy at birth are referred to as well, in order to illustrate the diversified mortality response to the transformation processes in central and eastern Europe (see Table 2 in the appendix).

Figure 2 – Elderly dependency ratio 2001

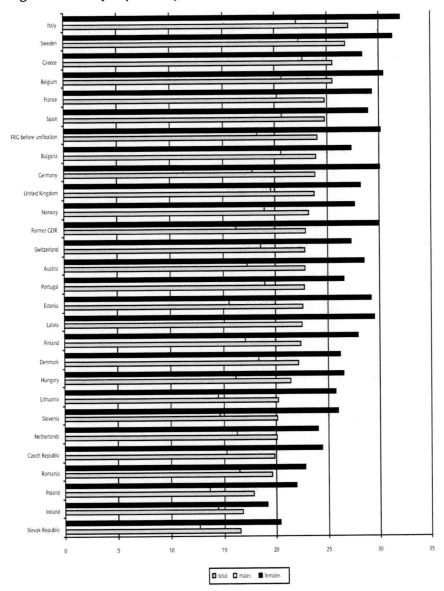

Source: Recent demographic developments in Europe, 2001, Council of Europe, own calculations.

All the countries studied experienced improvements in mortality from 1990-2000. However, the differences between western countries and transition countries still remained (e0) or even increased (e(45) and e(65)).

In western countries, increases in life expectancy at birth range between 1.3 (Greece) and 3.3 years (former GDR) for females (except for the Netherlands – the rise is only 0.5 years) and between 1.7 (Belgium, the Netherlands) and 3.2 years (Finland, former GDR) for males (except for Greece – the rise is only 0.8 year). Only in Greece, Portugal and Spain the female life expectancy increase is higher than for males.

A mortality decline can be observed in transition countries as well. The most significant rise in female life expectancy at birth occurs in the Czech Republic (2.9 years) and Poland (2.4 years), whereas the lowest increment is in Lithuania (1.4 years) and Bulgaria (0.4 years). Moreover, males born in 2000 are expected to live longer – the rise ranges between 0.5 (Bulgaria) and 4.1 years (the Czech Republic). Only in the Baltic countries and Romania are changes in life expectancy at birth for females more visible than those for males.

Significant changes have also occurred regarding life expectancy at age 45 and age 65. These changes differ markedly across two groups of countries. In western countries, males aged 45 are expected to live 1.3-2.5 years longer in 2000 than they were in 1990 (except for Greece – the rise is only 0.6 years) while females at that age are expected to live 0.9-2.7 years longer (except for the Netherlands – the rise is only by 0.3 year). Some transition countries experienced stagnation or even a drop in the life expectancy of males at age 45 (Bulgaria, Estonia, Romania, Latvia), whereas in others a diversified rise can be observed – from 0.52 years (Lithuania) to 3.1 years (the Czech Republic). Females aged 45 years are expected to live from 1-2.3 years longer. The lowest increase concerns females in Bulgaria (0.2) and Romania (0.7 year). As a result of these regional diversities, the gap between both groups of countries has been widening, especially for males.

Improvements in the life expectancy of males at age 65 are relatively small in southern Europe, France and the Netherlands (less than 1 year), while in other developed countries they exceed 1 year. Changes in that indicator for females are more diversified – from 0.3 years (the Netherlands) to 1.7 years (Austria) and 2.1 years (former GDR). In transition countries persons aged 65 years are generally supposed to live longer in 2000 than they were before. However, these changes differ across countries for both females and males. The Czech Republic is the leader (2.1 years for males and 1.8 years for females) followed by Poland (1.2 and 1.3 respectively) and Slovenia (0.8 and 1.6 respectively). The increases in the remaining countries range from 0.1-0.7 year for males and from 0.2-1.2 years for females.

These regional disparities in mortality changes in 1990-2000 contribute to marked differences in labour force and population ageing as well as to the future course both processes will take.

2.2. Projected changes in the working-age population

According to recent UN population projections (the 2000 revision), the total working-age population is expected to decline after 2010 (see Tables 3 and 4 in the appendix). In western countries, stabilisation around the level of 260 million in the years 2000-2010 will be followed by a decline of 4 million (1.3 %) in 2010-2015. In transition countries, after a slight increase (of around 1%), the labour supply is set to drop by 2.3 million (3.2%) in 2010-2015. The changes in the first decade regarding the labour supply increase will be most prevalent in Poland, and to a lesser extent in the Slovak Republic and Lithuania. In other countries the onset of the labour supply decline is expected either now, in the years 2000-2005, (Bulgaria, Hungary and Estonia) or in the period 2005-2010 (the Czech Republic, Romania and Slovenia).

Northern and north-western countries are set to see labour supply increase slowly, while Germany, Switzerland and southern countries are already confronted with a decline in this 2000-2005 period. In 2015 only Ireland and Norway will not experience a decline in labour supply, and five years later only Ireland will still be an exception.

Within a thirty year period the labour supply will decline by nearly 40.9 million, that is by 12% as compared to 2000. A continuation of that trend will lead to the working-age population in 2050 being 27% lower than in 2000.

The foreseen drop in labour supply is differentiated across countries and regions. The shrinking labour supply is expected to be more marked in transition countries, since the working-age population in that region will be lower in 2030 and 2050 than in 2000 by 14% and 33% respectively. These indices for western countries are 12% and 25%.

Up until 2030, Bulgaria, Estonia, Switzerland, Italy and Latvia will see their labour supplies decline by more than 20% as compared to 2000. Norway will maintain the 2000 level, while France will experience the smallest decline. Overall, the Baltic countries, central western Europe and southern Europe will be most seriously affected by the decline in the working-age population (by at least 17%).

On the other hand, the size of the population of those aged 55-64 is expected to rise by 35% until 2025 as compared to 2000, and most significantly in the years 2000-2015 (see Tables 5-6 in the appendix). However, both groups of countries differ in terms of the course their changes will take. In western countries the highest increase is set for the years 2015-2020. That population will, in 2025, reach the level of 59.25 million, that is 38% higher than in 2000. Later on, in 2050, the reversed trend will start to reach the size of the population which is 6% higher as compared to 2000. Transition countries will experience more irregular changes in terms of timing and direction: the rapid increase between 2005 and 2010, the continued rise until 2015 to 14 million people, that is 37% more than in 2000, the decline during the next decade, followed in 2025-2040 by another rise. Then in the last decade the number of persons aged 55-64 will drop again. In 2035 and 2040 that population will be 42%-44% higher than in 2000. In 2050 it is expected to be 20% higher than in 2000.

Figure 3 – Working-age population by regions, UN projections, medium variant

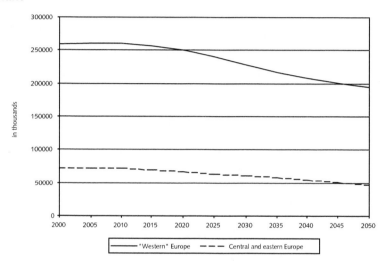

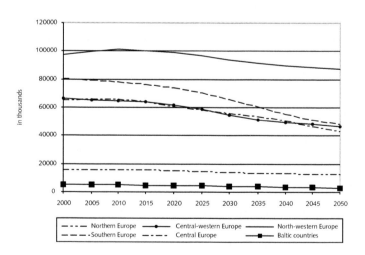

Source: own calculations based on data from World population prospects.The 2000 revision. Vol.II: Sex and age distribution of the world population, United Nations, New York 2001.

Looking at both groups of countries one can find considerable cross-region and cross-country differences. The population aged 55-64 years in central western and north-western Europe will see upward growth until 2025, and in southern Europe, until 2030. In central Europe this increase will cease by 2015.

Figure 4 – Population aged 55-64 by regions, UN projections, medium variant

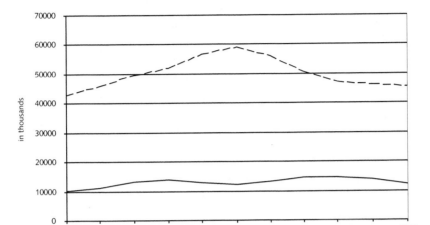

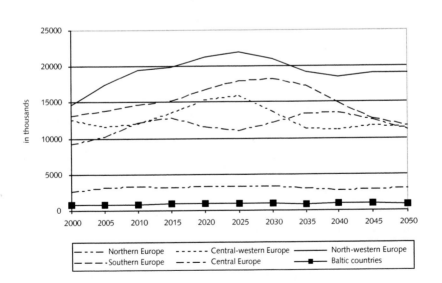

Source:own calculations based on data from World population prospects. The 2000 revision. Vol.II: Sex and age distribution of the world population, United Nations, New York, 2001.

Germany, Romania and the Baltic countries will see a decline in the number of older workers in the years 2000-2005. Northern Europe will experience a decline in the 2010-2015 period, like Bulgaria and the Czech Republic. For Finland, that fall will continue until 2035, in a similar way to Estonia and Latvia (see Tables 5-6 in the appendix).

Furthermore, the intensity of changes is markedly differentiated across countries. In the two decades to come, northern and north-western countries will be confronted with the most radical changes in the size of the older working population. For transition countries, the coming fifteen years will be key in that respect – Poland, the Czech Republic (until 2010), and the Slovak Republic will experience a rapid rise in the supply of older workers.

The changes described above are crucial for the timing of labour force ageing (see Table 7 and Figure 2.5). The process will intensify in northern and north-western countries, especially until 2010. In the next decade the central western part of Europe will be subjected to similar radical changes in the ageing indicator. The radical changes in the number of old persons of working-age predicted for central Europe will lead to the share of that population in 2010 being comparable with figures for north-western Europe. In 2020, the percentage of persons aged 55-64 will range between 20% (Portugal) and 26% (Switzerland) (Ireland is an outsider with 17%), while for transition countries it will range between 17% (Romania) and 23% (Slovenia). Ten years later that percentage will rise to 29% for Italy and 21% for Finland. In transition countries it will range between 20% for Poland and 25% for Slovenia. According to UN projections, from 2035 onwards the most accelerated ageing of the labour force can be expected in southern and central Europe.

The size of the population aged 65 and more is going to grow continuously in all countries and faster than that of the working-age population. In 2000, nearly 40% of European countries had 15% of their populations as old aged persons, whereas in 2015 the share of those countries is expected to grow to 60%. In 2030, almost all countries (95%) will belong to that group. Moreover, for the majority of them (75%), at least every fifth person will be aged 65 and more (Mašková, 2002). As a result the elderly dependency ratios will undergo an upward trend, especially after 2010.

In 2010, the number of elderly persons per 100 working-age persons is expected to range between 20 (central Europe) and 30 (central western Europe). Ten years after that the value below 30 will be relevant to transition countries only. In 2030, the lowest ratio is foreseen for central Europe (32), while the maximum value of 47 persons is foreseen for central western Europe). In the long run southern Europe and central western Europe will display that indicator most markedly.

Figure 5 – The percentage of persons aged 55-64 in the working-age population, UN projections, medium variant

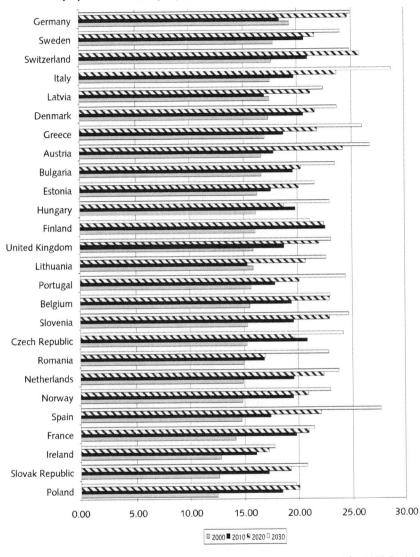

Source: own calculations based on data from World population prospects. The 2000 Revision. Vol.II: Sex and age distribution of the world population, United Nations, New York, 2001.

When looking at various countries one can notice that in 2030 Switzerland is set to be a leader (53 old persons per 100 of working-age people), followed by Italy, Austria, Germany, Sweden and Norway (46-47 persons). Only Ireland and Romania are predicted to have elderly dependency ratios of 26 persons.

Figure 6 – Elderly dependency ratio by regions, 2000-2050

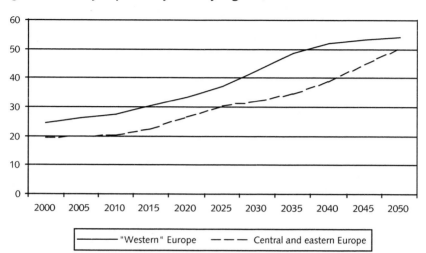

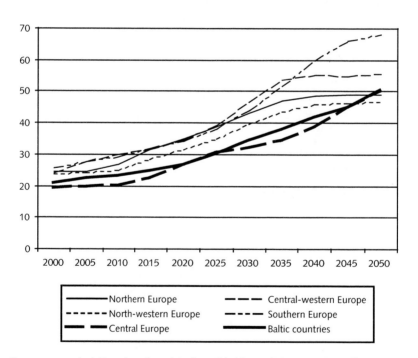

Source: own calculations based on data from World population prospects. The 2000 Revision. Vol II: Sex and age distribution of the world population, United Nations, New York, 2001.

Figure 7 – Elderly dependency ratio by countries, 2000-2050

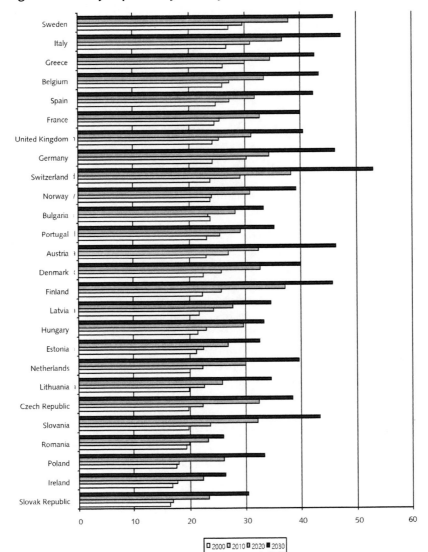

Source: own calculations based on data from World population prospects. The 2000 Revision. Vol II: Sex and age distribution of the world population, United Nations, New York, 2001.

2.3. Possible effects of the projected changes in the age composition

Predicted changes in the age composition show unfavourable shifts between the working-age population and the elderly population. Taking additionally into account the fact that effective dependency ratios, based on the relation between inactive and active populations, are considerably higher than measures currently discussed, and coupling that with labour force participation trends, which contribute to a worsening of effective ratios, concerns about the financial viability of public pension systems are deeply justified.

Moreover, shrinking working-age population and its ageing are expected to have widespread effects on the labour market and the economy. Firstly, the decreasing size of the working-age population may contribute to a decline in the labour force (employed and unemployed persons). If the current trends in the participation rates are to continue (baseline scenario), the labour force of the European Union will decline after 2010, and by 2050 the number of active people observed in 1985 might be reached (Statistics in focus, theme 1-2/ 2001, p.1). Despite regional differences in the timing and intensity of a decline, as well as differences in labour force participation, Europe will be confronted with a widespread labour force decline.

One can argue that the declining labour force might be counteracted by diminishing under-utilisation of labour, which is widespread across Europe. It seems, however, that labour force decline, coupled with its ageing, can result in labour force shortages and skill mismatches (especially in some regions and sectors of the economy), a slowdown of technological progress, as well as reduction in mobility and flexibility of the labour force. On the demand side, however, the increasing dynamics is observed, that is rapid technological change, profound shifts in work patterns (temporary jobs, part-time jobs, fragmentation of work and timing of work). The changing nature of employment from a structured work-life and work-environment to a self-managed, more flexible and personal career, might cause some difficulties for older workers. Therefore, there is cause for concern about the capabilities of labour supply, especially of older persons, to adapt to new requirements. Keeping in mind advances in population ageing and increasing old-age dependency ratios, as well as existing financial arrangements for pension systems, it can be concluded that on the whole Europe is confronted with a significant challenge to adjust labour market policies and social security systems to these changes.

3. Changes in the labour force participation rates of persons aged 55 and over

3.1. Overall trends in economic activity

Major changes in labour force participation since the 1970s are illustrated by the age-sex -specific labour force participation rates (LFPR) (see Table 8a and Table 8b in the appendix). Available data on a few transition countries for the years up to 1990 cannot be compared with data for the 1990s. Therefore, the long-term trends in LFPRs can only be analysed for western countries.

In western countries the LFPRs for males, especially for the age 55-64, reveal a general decrease in economic activity. The rates for males aged 25-49 being around the 90% level are homogenous across countries. Country differences increase within the age (Table 8a in the appendix). These changes cannot be associated only with economic cycles (for example an increase in the 1970s and a decline in the 1980s). Moreover, on the contrary, the economic activity of females has been continuously rising for those aged 25-54, especially aged 25-44 (Table 8b in the appendix). For the remaining age groups the changes did not show such a uniform picture. The increase can also be observed for females at age 55-59 (except for Austria) while the rates of females aged 60-64 declined (except for Sweden, Norway and Greece). The activity of females aged 65 was low and declined (Norway is again an exception).

Country heterogeneity with respect to the level of the female LFPRs is well-known. In 1970 the lowest rates were found in Italy, Greece, Belgium (around 30% for age 25-44) while the highest ones were found in Denmark, Austria and Sweden (around 50% for age 25-44). The differences still existed in the 1990s, but at the significantly higher level of economic activity: Italy and Greece are still at the bottom of the ranking list (61% and 66% for age 25-44), and Denmark, France, Norway and Sweden are at the top (81%-85%).

Women's participation in the labour market is expected to undergo a further increase associated with favourable changes in the labour market (development of services, more flexible work patterns), increases in human capital of women (increasing school enrolment), and changes in the social and cultural environment (changes in values and norms).

Centrally planned economies had, by European standards, a high economic activity for both males and females. These countries were almost uniform in terms of LFPRs of males and slightly differentiated in terms of females' rates. In fact, that measure can be compared with employment rates for the developed market economies, given the full-employment principle and a lack of open unemployment before the 1990s.

Labour market participation changed drastically under the transition to a market economy. In most of the transition countries economic reforms brought a sharp contraction in output and employment accompanied by a rise in unemployment. Despite the recovery, which started in around 1993, employment has continued to decline or stagnate. The LFPRs, available from labour force surveys,[15] fell in all countries, most visibly in Bulgaria, Hungary and Poland. However, as compared to the EU-15 participation rates in

---

15.The national labour force surveys were introduced in transition countries in the first half of the 1990s, according to international recommendations on definitions and methods. They have become the main source of data on labour market developments. A selection of transition countries forming part of that study has been based on the availability of comparative labour market data. Among ten countries selected, Hungary was the first country, with the survey established in 1991, and Latvia and Estonia were the last ones with the surveys starting in 1995.

1996, in most transition countries they were still higher than the EU average (67.7%). Lower rates were found for Bulgaria and Poland (central European countries' employment and labour market review, 1999). Slowing economic growth at the end of the 1990s was accompanied by further employment decline and a rise in unemployment.

The contraction in demand for labour, along with the growing working-age population has put strong pressure upon the labour market, reflected in high unemployment in most countries. In 2000, unemployment rates below 10% were observed only in Romania and Hungary. Youth and female unemployment were above average. To deal with rising unemployment governments liberalised disability and early retirement provision. As a result, economic activity of persons aged 55-64 dropped considerably.

3.2. Changes in the labour force participation of persons aged 55 and over

The general downward trend in the LFPRs of persons aged 55 and more is markedly differentiated by countries. The regional differences in 2000 are illustrated by data in Table 9. It is important to remember, however, that in western countries the trend results mainly from declining labour force participation of males, while in transition countries declines in both male and female economic activity contributed to the observed change. The declining labour force participation of older workers is most commonly due to: increased living standards of the population, incentives embedded in social security systems, and labour market structures (for example Blöndal and Scarpetta, 1999a, 1999b; Gruber and Wise, 1999; Disney and Whitehouse, 1999a, 1999c; OECD, 1995a, 1995b). The intensity of changes across age groups is affected by the different standard age of retirement by countries as well.

Despite the fact that in most western countries the standard age of retirement for males, being at least 65 years, (France, Greece and Italy are exceptions), was relatively stable over time, economic activity rates of males aged 55-59 range from 54% (Italy) to 89% (Sweden) and those of males aged 60-64 from 5% (Spain) to 84% (Sweden) (Table 9 and Table 10).

The relatively rapid changes in economic activity of older workers in transition countries led to the LFPRs of males being considerably lower when compared to the developed economies (Table 9). However, it should be noted that the standard age of retirement is, for both males and females, lower than in western countries – on average 60 years for males and 57 for females (Table 11).

Changes in the labour market participation of older workers can also be illustrated by employment rates. The data in Table 12 show the general downward trend of employment rates up to 1995 and a relatively high degree of under-utilisation of persons aged 55-64. In 1995 only Denmark, Norway, Sweden, Switzerland had employment rates which were not lower than 50%. It seems that this trend was stopped in some countries at the end of the 1990s. However, that change is combined with a higher incidence of long-term unemployment among persons in older ages in most countries (Table 14). Unemployment rates do not incorporate the higher unemployment risk among persons in immobile age – that is, persons in working age (as defined by internal country regulations) aged 45 and more – but if these persons become unemployed the threat of long-term unemployment is significantly higher.

3.3. Possible determinants of declining economic activity of persons aged 55 and over

Labour market related effects and institutional factors are highlighted as the main determinants of the developments of economic activity of older workers in western countries. In empirical studies both the demand effect (structure of the economy, high and persistent unemployment, technological progress) and the supply effect (the size and age composition of the labour force, old-age pensions and other non-employment related benefits) are usually analysed. Here, two comparative studies are directly referred to. The study on determinants of changes in the labour force participation rates of older men by Blöndal and Scarpetta (1999a) is based on data about fifteen OECD countries from the years 1971-1995. The analysis of labour force participation rates of both females and males aged 55-74 by Vlasblom and Nekkers (2001) refers to the European Union countries at the national and regional (NUTS-II) levels and covers the period 1992-1997.

The main findings by Blöndal and Scarpetta (1999a) can be summarised as follows:

- there is a close correlation between the average effective retirement age and continued work;

- pension wealth accrual and unemployment-related benefits have a strong impact on decisions to retire;

- the availability of generous non-employment benefits seems to be a prerequisite for labour market variables to influence activity rates of older workers;

- the labour market variables play a significant role in explaining cross-country and time variations in the economic activity of older men: the increase in the prime-age unemployment rate influences the drop in the labour force participation rate, changes in the size and the age composition of the working-age population seem to exert strong pressure for early withdrawal on older male workers;

- institutional factors like different bargaining systems (the level of centralisation/co-ordination of wage negotiations) and the degree of unionisation (the share of trade union members) play direct and indirect roles: for example high levels of unionisation have favoured early withdrawals by promoting early retirement schemes at the firm and/or sectoral level, and the stronger effect of changes in the labour supply on participation rates was found in countries with sectoral bargaining but without co-ordination;

- labour market factors and institutional factors explain a great deal of the cross-country and time-series differences in the labour force participation rates, however a large part of the cross-country variation remains unexplained.

In the study on changes in economic activity rates by Vlasblom and Nekkers (2001), the labour supply factors were represented by age, gender and education, while labour demand factors by employment variables: employment structure (agriculture, industry, services), employment status (employees, self-employed), and full-time and part-time workers. Institutional factors were reflected in a set of dummy variables on the pension systems, including the standard age of retirement, a possibility to defer pension, a possibility to retire early, partial pension arrangements. The main empirical results can be synthesised as follows:

- more higher educated persons tend to stay longer in the labour market;

- the higher the pension age, the higher the activity rates;

- the possibility to defer pensions increases the activity rates;

- the possibility of early retirement lowers the activity rates of males younger than 65 and increases the rates of males older than 65;

- a similar effect has been noted regarding the possibility to use a partial pension.

Both studies confirm that the majority of the differences in the labour force participation rates between countries stem from differences in the country-specific labour force behaviour (behaviour and work attitudes) and institutional and policy factors affecting labour supply decisions. Moreover, attempts by Vlasblom and Nekkers (2001) at finding groups of countries with similar patterns of interrelations between the economic activity of older workers and variables related to demographic, educational and economic structures show that there is no clear subdivision in countries where either demographics or educational and economic structures has the greatest influence. These results confirm the relevance of contextual factors for such studies.

The decline in economic activity of persons aged 55 and over in transition countries could also be related to both the demand and supply sides. The demand for labour has been strongly influenced by the transformation processes: institutional changes linked to the establishment of a labour market and the restructuring of the economy and employment structures. Economic reforms imposed a fundamental reconstruction of labour market control mechanisms aimed at the more effective management of the work-force, a rise in labour productivity and an improvement in the quality of work. Demand for labour changed drastically in quantitative and qualitative terms. On the supply side the increase in the size of the working-age population and its ageing and declining spatial mobility were observed. Moreover, the fact that the overwhelming majority of older workers were low-skilled significantly reduced their capacity to avoid skill mismatches. Demand-supply imbalances led to rising unemployment in most countries on a large and unanticipated scale. Moreover, the strategy to re-allocate some groups of the population from work to outside the labour market was frequently used to limit the labour supply (for example liberalising entitlements to early retire-ment and implementing non-employment related benefits). However, these changes have not been as well documented in empirical studies as those in developed European economies, or at least until now. The employment rates of persons aged 55-64 are somewhat lower than in western countries and seem to undergo further decline in most countries (Table 13).[16] The incidence of long-term unemployment among those persons, lower than for the total population, indicate that applied measures to withdraw them from the labour force have worked quite efficiently (Table 14). However, that policy resulted in the rapid increase in the size of the inactive population. In the space of a few years the pension system dependency ratio (pensioners to contributors) grew drastically.

4. Old-age pension systems and incentives to early retirement

The early withdrawal of older workers from the labour market is shown not only by the declining economic activity rates of those people, but also by the drop in the effective retirement age. In practice, most people retire before the standard pension age. The effective retirement age is on average five years lower.

Possible reasons behind early retirement developments include the following:

- increased affluence and higher incomes could have increased the demand for leisure;

---

16. Recent studies based on the LFS data in Poland seem to indicate a worsening of the labour market situation of older workers in the years 1997-2000. Their possibilities to be active (to be employed) declined in comparison to the reference age group (30-34 for males and 40-44 for females). Furthermore, higher education improves their chances of staying in the labour market (Boroń, 2002).

- imbalances in the labour market which put older workers at a disadvantage in competitions for jobs;

- the expansion of occupational pension schemes, voluntarily negotiated between employers and employees, could, in some countries, lead to early departures from the labour market as being an attractive option for workers;

- the increase in the financial incentives for early retirement embedded in public social security systems, including old-age pensions and other non-employment benefits (see for instance Blöndal and Scarpetta, 1999b, Disney and Whitehouse, 1999c, Gruber and Wise, 1999).

Before the discussion on financial incentives for early retirement in the public social security systems, the main features of public old-age pension systems are presented. The overview of the public systems is supplemented by brief information on private pension schemes. That part of the report is mainly based on publications by Blöndal and Scarpetta (1999a), Disney and Whitehouse (1999c), Gruber and Wise (1999), and Kalisch and Aman (1998).

4.1. Main features of old-age pension systems

Retirement policies could be considered in terms of the old-age pension programmes existing in European countries. There are different typologies of pension systems. What seems to be important for the purpose of the study is to look at schemes managed by public entities with a high level of national level co-ordination, and more precisely, to concentrate on public defined-benefit pension schemes since, despite the fact that schemes with defined contributions are playing a bigger role (for example reforms in transition countries, and in Italy and Sweden), they have been developed recently and relatively few people have retired by these schemes. The issue of retirement incentives in these pension plans has not yet been addressed in the relevant studies. In fact, the schemes with national level co-ordination are regarded as public schemes in the national accounts system even if they are primarily managed by private entities.

Under the public defined-benefit pension systems two types of pension plans are developed: flat-rate basic pension schemes and earnings-related pension schemes. Flat-rate basic pension schemes aim at ensuring the minimum level of income for the elderly. Their funding is tax-based or contribution-based. The eligibility requirements are often: age, a certain length of the residence in the country, and a means test. They are called social pensions in some countries (for example Italy has changed the name of its social pension to social allowance).

Earnings-related pension schemes are primarily intended to raise the income of retired persons. In those countries which have the flat-rate basic pension schemes the earnings-related pension schemes often serve as the second tier of the whole structure of pension programmes. In these pension schemes the level of benefit is related to the income earned before retirement. Their funding is usually contribution-based (with state subsidies in some cases). Eligibility requirements refer to: age, a certain length of employment or vesting period in which the insured pays contributions.

There exists a great variety of pension plans developed under the public defined-benefit pension schemes. To compare them one should consider the following components of the pension plans:

- coverage;
- the method of final benefit calculation which varies considerably between countries;
- an accrual structure of the scheme – different accrual factors are used for different years (non-linear structure);[17]
- earnings measure in the public defined-benefit pension schemes;[18]
- actuarial adjustments to defined-benefit pensions: they aim to reflect the fact that the pensions are drawn either early or late;
- counting or neglecting periods outside the labour force (non-contributory periods);
- the existence of some elements of income redistribution: a maximum limit on earnings to be used for calculations;[19]
- earning while drawing pension;[20]
- indexation of final benefits – based on price inflation or wage growth;
- tax concessions.[21]

---

17. Usually a higher accrual rate is used for early years of contributions. As later years have a lower return to working, this can be a disincentive to continue work. Other schemes have a maximum pension level or a maximum number of years of accrual in the plan.

18. Three main solutions are used (Disney and Whitehouse, 1999c, 19):
- average earnings across all or most of the working life (for example Belgium, Germany, UK)
- the number of the "best" years (for example Norway – 20, Austria –15, Sweden – 15, France – 11)
- final few years of the working life, for example the Czech Republic, Portugal (best 10 of 15), Hungary (best 4 of 5), Poland (6 of final 15).

19. Solutions adopted aim to provide a higher replacement rate for former lower income earners as well as to constrain the benefit available to those earning high incomes.

20. The possibilities to combine work and pensions are highly differentiated between countries, ranging from no restrictions (Finland, Germany, the Netherlands, UK, Sweden, as in 1998) to a full withdrawal (Spain, Portugal, Austria, Belgium) (Disney and Whitehouse, 1999c, 27). Partial retirement programmes (that is the possibility to cut hours of work while claiming part of the pension) could be considered as one possible solution: for instance, in Denmark people who reduce their working time between 60 and the standard age of retirement (67) can receive part of their pension.

21. In some countries pensioners are treated more generously than workers, for example in Austria 75% of pension annuity income is tax-free, pension income is tax-free in Hungary, the Czech Republic, and pensioners do not have to pay contributions to the health care services in Italy.

The public defined-benefit pension systems are predominantly based on a PAYG basis that is contributions and tax revenues from the current working population are used to fund the retirement benefits of the currently retired population. In the PAYG scheme contributions paid serve a dual purpose: to contribute towards the pension payments of the current retired population as well as to establish the future pension rights of the contributors.

The decline in the economic activity of older workers, accompanied by the population ageing as well as the labour force ageing, cause deep concern about the financial viability of public pension systems due to the rising imbalance between the number of the contributors to these systems and their benefi-ciaries. In transition countries shrinking tax bases additionally affect public pension finances. The subjects of policy concern are also: low effective retire-ment age, work disincentives embedded in the pension systems, adequacy of the pension benefit level (mostly in transition countries), and improving the size of population covered by pension arrangement (based on the OECD caring world questionnaire).

The level of pension benefit related to the prior earnings of workers is meas-ured by the replacement rate. According to ILO Convention No. 102 from 1952, public old-age pension schemes should ensure a replacement rate (RR) of at least 40% for a couple of pensionable age. The overview compiled by Kalisch and Aman (1998) shows that most OECD countries meet that recom-mendation.

Concerns about the financial viability of public pension systems are one of many reasons for looking for other financial arrangements for pensions. One possibility is private pension schemes, which are becoming more significant in the whole scheme of pension income provision. They aim to provide saving mechanisms for old age and to encourage long-term savings.

Forms of private saving and their relations with public pensions are different across countries. Private pension schemes may be limited to particular labour force groups (by occupation, industries, work contract, etc.). Private savings may be available to supplement a public pension or substitute for that ben-efit. Disregarding forms and links to the public pension scheme, the private financial arrangements for pensions have common features (Kalisch, Aman, 1998, p.14): they are mostly based on voluntary participation, almost exclu-sively fully-funded, and predominantly supplement the public pension. The eligibility age for final benefits is often lower than the standard age of retire-ment. However, some restrictions on early access could be implemented. They are formulated as a mix of the defined-benefit and defined contribution schemes. Private pension savings usually receive some form of government financial subsidy (via the tax system) and regulatory protection. Along with growing overall welfare as well as individual concerns about future pensions these schemes are set to become more important.

4.2. Incentives to early retirement embedded in the social security system

Theoretical considerations as well as empirical studies demonstrate that defined-benefit pension schemes include work disincentives (for example Blöndal and Scarpetta, 1999a, 1999b; Gruber and Wise, 1999; Kalisch, Aman, 1998; Disney and Whitehouse, 1999a, 1999c). Here, the reference is made to a theoretical approach by Disney and Whitehouse (1999c) and the extended empirical study by Blöndal and Scarpetta (1999a).

Disney and Whitehouse (1999c), using the theoretical model of optimal retirement of the defined-benefit pension scheme, indicate the following work disincentives, which result from the logic of that scheme:

- early retirement programmes that enable people to stop working with no reduction in pension or a decrement that is less than actuarially fair;

- non-linear accrual structures or maximum pensions that give a low or zero increment to pensions for working when older;

- final salary formulae that encourage people to leave the labour market once earnings reach their peak (age-profile of earnings);

- earning tests that prevent people from combining work and pensions;

- non-actuarially fair increments for deferring a pension claim;

- pension systems that still levy employer and/or employee contributions even when no additional pension is earned.

The findings of the study on financial incentives to early retirement in the public social security systems over the past three decades in OECD countries by Blöndal and Scarpetta (1999a) confirm that evaluation of defined-benefit pension systems. They developed a new analytical framework for the public social security systems (old-age pension systems, disability, unemployment-related and special early-retirement programmes), which aims at taking into account different rules applied in the real pension systems. Its components are: expected old-age pension wealth for a single worker at different retirement ages, retirement incentives – changes in pension wealth resulting from postponing retirement by one year, and the implicit tax rate expected at age x for one more year of work (the difference between costs and benefits of continued work at given age relative to expected gross earnings).

Some results of that study are given in Tables 16-20 in the appendix. Of special interest is the notable increase in the implicit tax on work after age 55 over recent decades (Table 20), caused by the lowering of the standard retirement age, higher pension replacement rates, flatter pension accruals at older ages, and higher pension contribution rates.

The summary of their findings may be formulated as follows (p.9):

* old-age pension systems discourage work at older ages in virtually all OECD countries. These disincentives are particularly strong after the earliest age at which pensions become available: continued work typically implies foregone pensions and continued payment of pension contributions with little or no increase in ultimate pensions after retirement;

* in those countries where other income support schemes can be accessed prior to the standard pension age, financial incentives to early retirement are amplified: the cost of an extra year of work is not only paid contributions but also foregone benefits, whereas ultimately pensions are often unaffected;

* the schemes originally designed to deal with unemployment or disability are used to finance early retirement. They operate within disability programmes, notably where a labour market criterion is explicitly used to assess entitlement to benefits, and unemployment-related programmes.[22] Moreover, in several countries early-retirement programmes have been established to assist older people to retire before the pensionable age;

* the difference in the average age across countries is closely related to the extent of the disincentives. According to estimated results from pooled cross-country time-series regression, removing these disincentives could lead to an increase in the labour force participation rates of older males (55-64) of almost 10 percentage points in those countries where the financial penalties are particularly high.

Some of these results, empirically justified for western countries, are also relevant for developments in transition countries. In particular early retirement arrangements, which were extended in the 1990s, as well as disability and unemployment-related programmes aimed, in fact, at diminishing labour market imbalances and easing the social and political costs of restructuring the economy. The ratio of pensioners to contributors has grown drastically. For instance in Romania and Bulgaria they reached 100% recently, that is each worker has to support one beneficiary (Rutkowski, 2002b). Changes in the number of contributors were even more negative than those on the expenditure side, which have been affected by the rising beneficiary population.

22.For instance, such regulations like an extension of the benefit period for older persons to the standard age of retirement, the removal of the job-search requirement for older workers, and the establishment of unemployment pensions. The relevance of unemployment and disability schemes to strengthen early retirement incentives has also been indicated by Kapteyn and de Vos (1998) and Kerkhofs et al.(1999) (in Van Dalen and Henkens, 2002).

The contribution base has shrunk dramatically. The main reasons for that change were: the decline in economic activity, changes in the labour force composition: an increasing number of self-employed and private firms were acting in the informal economy, and also the growing debts of state enterprises. What happened in transition countries with PAYG schemes demonstrates clearly the sensitivity of that scheme to changes in the labour market (Augusztinovics, 1999, after Fultz, Ruck, 2001), contrary to its usual perception as dependent on demographic factors.

To counteract the deterioration of public pension finances some amendments to the PAYG schemes were implemented. For instance, a ceiling on the maximum pension (Hungary and Poland), a new flat component coupled with the earning-related component reduced in size (Lithuania and Estonia), *ad hoc* changes in the benefit formula (Romania and Bulgaria), and a focus on price indexation instead of full wage indexation aimed at compressing the benefit structure to control expenditures. Moreover, the elimination of occupational privileges and a rise in the statutory retirement age were accepted as appropriate measures (Rutkowski, 2002b). However, it became more and more clear that fundamental changes were needed to ensure the financial sustainability of pension systems given the predicted advancement in population and labour force ageing.

5. Reforms of pension systems and the economic activity of older workers

A recapitulation of the discussions outlined in the previous sections provides a picture of the challenges faced by pension systems both in western and transition countries. Both groups of countries are characterised by low ratios of pensioners to contributors, rising average replacement rates and a relatively low retirement age despite increasing life expectancy. Pension systems in transition countries are additionally facing specific problems which result mainly from the pension schemes existing before the transition, as well as the economic and institutional problems generated by the transition to a market economy. The major differences between the two groups of countries are certain features of the schemes in transition countries: universal coverage ensured by state-owned industries, benefit and eligibility based on full employment/compressed wage, less significant indexation, weak contribution collection and recording, decentralisation of administrative systems, and low reliance on private pensions (see for instance Kalisch and Aman, 1998; Chłoń, Góra, and Rutkowski, 1999; Rutkowski, 1998, 2002a, 2002b).

Reforms recently undertaken in several countries or/and those still to be implemented put the highest priority on the medium and long-term financial viability of public pension systems, funded predominantly on a PAYG basis. That issue is related to the potential burden of future generations to fund the public pension systems. Other commonly listed goals of intended reforms are:

- reducing pension generosity;
- removing financial incentives to early retirement;
- improving the adequacy of pension benefit levels;
- increasing the number of contribution years;
- increasing the share of the population covered by pension arrangements;
- promoting private pension schemes, and
- getting greater convergence between existing public and private pension schemes.

There is no single measure used for the purpose of pension reform. Among measures suggested, those promoting the economic activity of older workers are ones we are focusing on (see Kalisch, Aman, 1998; Disney and White-house, 1999c, *La protection sociale dans les états membres de l'UE et de L'Espace Economique Européen, situation au 1er janvier 2001, Commission Européene*, MISSOC 2001). For example :

- a reduction in early retirement opportunities by an actuarial reduction in early–retirement pensions, an increase in the standard age of retirement, tighter conditions for entitlement (duration of employment, participation in training programmes);
- some disincentives to work in the defined-benefit scheme can be mitigated by moving to pensions based on the average salary across the working life rather than on a limited number of best or final years. Maximum pensions and limits to the number of years of contributions that earn pensions should be removed;
- permission to combine pensions at the standard age with some work;
- the introduction of partial retirement schemes aimed at helping people leave the workforce gradually by moving to part-time work;
- equalising women's retirement age.

Table 11 provides data on changes in the standard age of retirement in transition countries. Similar policy initiatives, especially with respect to women's age, have also been undertaken by other countries, for example, Italy: from 63 to 65 for men and 58 to 60 for women (by 2000); 57-65 in new scheme, Austria: from 60 to 65 in the years 2019-2028 for females, Belgium: from 62 to 65 in the years 1997-2009, Greece: from 60 to 65 for the post-1993 labour-market entrants, Portugal: to 65 by 1999 for females, Switzerland: from 62 to 64 (by 2005), remains below men's age of 65, United Kingdom:

from 60 to 65 (by 2020). According to the proposed regulation in Sweden, employees would stay in employment until 67 (Kalisch, Aman, 1998; OECD, 2001b).

Examples of other measures counteracting early retirement are: Austria has implemented a programme of reduced access to early retirement, Belgium will increase contribution years for retirement at 60 from 20 to 35 (by 2005), Greece has introduced minimum contribution years from 13.5 to 15, Portugal has increased the minimum contribution years from 10 to 15, and France from 37.5 to 40 years, Italy has set the minimum age at 52 (from 1997) and the contribution years from 35 to 40 years (from 2008). Finland introduced a lower benefit and increased minimum age from 55 to 58, similarly in Germany the minimum age will increase to 62 (from 2012). New regulations in Norway provide for a smaller reduction for working while drawing pension for ages 67-70, in Sweden and United Kingdom they allow for actuarial increases for deferral after the age of 70.

The Netherlands have introduced radical reform of the early-retirement system by switching from the PAYG schemes to more actuarially neutral ones. Under the new regime the early-retirement benefit is related directly to the work record and the contribution paid, accumulated on an individual basis. The minimum retirement age is 55 (van Dalen and Henkens, 2002).

Altogether, measures to be introduced and those already implemented aim not only at encouraging older workers to stay in the labour market but also at a smooth transition from work to retirement, which enables persons below the statutory retirement age to reduce their workload.

In discussions on how to adapt pension schemes to demographic and labour market challenges, the issue of closer links between benefits and contributions remains one of the main problems. What is an adequate solution: to reform defined-benefit schemes or to introduce notional defined contribution schemes? A reform strategy oriented at the first option could include a reformulated benefit structure (for example by adjusting the contribution rate, the pension coverage ratio and the replacement rate, reducing the accrual periods, lengthening the assessment periods, introducing actuarially fair adjustments for late/early retirements, and incorporating demographic and fiscal factors in the benefit formula). Early retirement should be eliminated or permitted on a more limited and actuarially fair basis. Also consolidation of the system by removing sector privileges and administrative adjustments is necessary. With that approach changes in some parameters of the system are implemented, however, its logic remains unchanged. As noted by Rutkowski (2002b), these adjustments can be termed parametric reforms. They are adopted by many developed countries.

Scheme 1 – Pension reforms in transition economies (multi-pillar system)

Country	Starting date	First pillar*	Size of the second pillar as share of payroll	Projected pension fund assets in 2020 (% GDP)	Workforce in funded pillar (2003)	Switching strategy
Hungary Legislated and operating	January 1998	PAYG DB	6%	31%	45%	Mandatory new entrants Voluntary others
Poland Legislated and operating	January 1999	NDC	7.2%	33%	70%	Mandatory < 30, Voluntary 30-50
Latvia Legislated and operating	July 2001 (NDC January 1996)	NDC	2% growing to 9%	20%	72%	Mandatory <30, Voluntary 30-50
Croatia Legislated	January 2003	PAYG DB	5%	25%-30%	60-70%	Mandatory <40, Voluntary 40-50
Bulgaria Legislated and operating	January 2002	PAYG DB	2% growing to 5%			Mandatory <42
Estonia Legislated	July 2002	PAYG DB	6%	20%	60%	Voluntary (opt-out +2%)
Romania Partially legislated then questioned	January 2003	PAYG DB	8%	30%	75%	Mandatory > 20 years from retirement
"The former Yugoslav Republic of Macedonia" Legislated	August 2002	PAYG DB	7%	26%	15%	Mandatory New entrants

*PAYG DB – pay-as-you-go defined-benefit scheme; NDC – notional defined contribution scheme.
Source: Rutkowski, M. 2002. "Strategic choices in pension reform in central and eastern Europe and Central Asia", the paper presented at the World Bank seminar, Białobrzegi, Poland, March 2002.

Moving towards a notional defined contribution scheme requires a transformation of the public pension system into a new system based on individual accounts. Pension contributions are credited with an "interest rate" equal to growth in the country's aggregate wage. Each person's pension depends on his or her accumulated amount divided up by the average life expectancy at the retirement age. That formula uses lifetime wages to determine benefits, includes adjustments to growing longevity and incentives for older workers to remain in the labour force and pay contributions. Sweden, Italy, Latvia and Poland are examples of this approach, which imposes a change in the paradigm of the system. These paradigmatic reforms (Rutkowski, 2002b) encourage not only those below the standard retirement age but also persons above that age to stay in the labour market.

The reforms of the pension systems undertaken in most of the transition countries apply both strategies. For instance, Poland and Latvia have implemented the paradigmatic reforms while other countries have applied the parametric approach. The scheme given below illustrates ideas used to change pension systems in transition countries.

It is difficult to state definitely whether the parametric or paradigmatic approach is better when reforming pension systems given the existing and future challenges. The parametric reforms improve the short-term financial stability of the system but for the long-term sustainability further changes are needed. Furthemore, diversification of pension provisions proceeds much slower than under paradigmatic reforms. Incentives to stay longer in the labour market seem to be weaker. Placing more emphasis on the individual responsibility for the future pensions in the paradigmatic reform is also its advantage. Altogether, the move towards financial stability is mentioned as an advantage of the changing paradigm solution, however, high transition costs are pointed out as its drawback (for example World Bank, *Averting the old age crisis,* 1994; Disney, 1999; Disney, Whitehouse, 1999b; Rutkowski, 2002b).

6. Concluding remarks

Recent population projections by the UN (World population prospects, 2001) and labour force projections by Eurostat (Statistics in focus, 2001) show clearly that population ageing, the decline in the labour force and its ageing are unavoidable characteristics of the Europe of the future. The pressure on the social security system, which results from these changes, and especially on those pension systems predominantly based on the PAYG basis, is additionally affected by labour market developments. The labour market imbalances contribute to increases in system dependency ratios.

With these future population trends – on one hand – and the high degree of under-utilisation of labour force widespread across Europe – on the other, the logical question to be asked is if there will be an increase in demand for labour, and can that increase be met by increased economic activity rates (Pearce and Punch, 2000, p.11)? The report focuses on possible changes in labour market participation of older workers that is of the persons aged 55 years and more, the group in the labour force which has experienced the most significant decline in economic activity over recent decades. That change significantly affects the negative shifts between contributors and recipients of the pension systems.

A concern about deteriorating levels of income support for the elderly, which was widely shared by the governments, has led to many policy initiatives aimed at improving social and private financial arrangements for retirement, increasing labour force participation of older workers and establishing a closer link between contributions and benefits. In the report the main emphasis has been placed on those initiatives which remove incentives to early retirement. Two main strategies for a pension system reform, described here, are dealing with incentives to stay longer in the labour market.

Retirement reforms are the most recent to be implemented. To what extent will decisions taken on retirement change? What might be the other effects of the longer stay of older workers in employment? It must be remembered that under-utilisation of productive capacity and unemployment are widespread across Europe. Early retirement regulations as well as occupational pension arrangements have been implemented to facilitate the exit of older workers to combat youth unemployment. Under existing labour market structures, reduced opportunities in early retirement could lead to a rise in disability incidence and unemployment (see for instance van Dalen and Henkens, 2002). Therefore, changes in the old-age pension system need to be combined with other income-support programmes. Moreover, the removal of disincentives to work longer would significantly increase the supply of older workers in the labour market. It might be difficult to absorb this increase in countries with high structural unemployment.

Furthermore, existing employers' attitudes towards older workers would limit the effects of measures stimulating their higher labour market participation. Research among employers carried out in several European countries has shown that they still do not consider older workers a force to be reckoned with. Few employers are inclined to recruit older workers due to a perceived lack of appropriate skills, a truncated payback period on training, and rules governing company/occupational pension schemes. On the contrary, many employers prefer laying off older workers first when firms downsize their labour force instead of implementing programmes to retain and retrain them (Henkens, van Dalen, forthcoming; Taylor, 2002). Moreover, employers perceive increasing labour costs as one of the most important effects of labour force ageing, because wages increase more with age than productivity. Additionally, older workers might be negatively affected by technological progress, which erodes their technology's specific human capital. They could also have some difficulties in adapting to new work patterns. To sum up, new policies to encourage older workers to stay in employment often do not coincide with reforms aimed at improving working conditions for older workers and increasing their employment prospects (Taylor, 2001, from van Dalen and Henkens, 2002). Without measures which stimulate employers to employ older workers these policies will be less effective. Moreover, financial incentives for firms seem to be insufficient as attempts undertaken in some countries demonstrate (such as wage subsidies and reducing social security contributions for firms) (see for instance OECD, 2001a). The issue is much more complex.

A need for urgent retirement reforms is perceived mostly at the macro level. On the level of organisations and individuals, and also among older workers, the problem is not considered to be so important. Moreover, besides the determinants mentioned above, the attitudes by employers are also affected by norms and representations of age and stereotypes concerning younger and older workers in the labour market. For many years, a prevailing view was that in combating unemployment among young people older workers were supposed to make room for young workers on the labour market. Therefore, much more should be done to raise awareness of the issue of ageing, employment and links to retirement systems. National education programmes have been undertaken in many countries (Taylor, 2001 in van Dalen and Henkens, 2002; Taylor, 2002). Despite their mixed and questionable effects until now, it seems to be reasonable to expect some changes in opinions at least in mid-term, especially under conditions to combine them with educational programmes and supporting local job initiatives aimed to strengthen the position of older workers within firms and in the labour market.[23]

Policies stimulating labour market participation of older workers should be considered within a framework of the broad economic and social policy reforms needed to adapt to population ageing, the labour force decline and the ageing labour force. All relevant actors from different levels should be involved. The effectiveness of encouraging older people to stay in the labour market depends largely "on the extent to which labour market conditions will make the older worker an essential part of the work force. Of course,

---

23. Taylor (2002) is of the opinion that educational campaigns among private sector small and medium-sized enterprises with a local emphasis, that focus on individual companies and organisations, sectors or occupational groups directly, will be more effective than broadly focused educational campaigns.

not only governments, employers organisations and unions need to acknowledge the vital position of the older worker for the present and future work force, but also the individual employers and employees should start perceiving this" (Henkens, van Dalen, forthcoming).

A similar view is presented by Blöndal and Scarpetta (1999b, pp. 41-42): "the adjustment would be eased if reforms of pensions and other income-support systems for the elderly were to be accompanied by measures to increase job opportunities in general, including elimination of measures and practices that discriminate against the hiring and training of older workers (OECD, 1998). The reforms discussed above could themselves contribute to increasing job opportunities for older workers, by inducing, *inter alia*, changes in their wage determination, participation in training, mobility and working-hour schedules. However, more broad-based reforms of labour and product markets along the lines advocated in the OECD job strategy would make transition to increase participation of older workers in the labour market both easier and quicker".

Taylor (2002) points out that pension and welfare reforms have dominated policies on older workers to date. Comprehensive or strategic approaches to employment and retirement of older workers, which aim at integrating older workers in the labour market, as well as at closing down options to early exits, have been implemented only in a few countries (Austria, Finland and United Kingdom). In other European countries fragmented policies affecting older workers prevail (Taylor, 2002, p. 12). For example:

• active labour market programmes targeting older workers (Austria, Belgium, Denmark, Finland, France, Germany, Greece, Ireland, the Netherlands and United Kingdom);

• wage subsidy schemes and other employment incentive schemes (Austria, Belgium, Denmark, Finland, France, Germany, Greece, Italy, Luxembourg, Netherlands, Spain and United Kingdom);

• support to employers (for example, advice and guidance, training, employment placements – Denmark, Finland and United Kingdom);

• age discrimination legislation, protection against dismissal, proscription of age bars in recruitment advertisements, and/or abolition of mandatory retirement (Austria, Belgium, Finland, France, Ireland, Italy, Spain and United Kingdom);

• awareness raising campaigns among employers (Denmark, Finland, Germany, Netherlands and United Kingdom).

He also shares the view on the need for integrating pension and social welfare reforms and employment policy. "Without an integrated and nuanced approach which brings together all relevant actors in government, the social partners and the not-for-profit sector it will be difficult to make significant progress in tackling age and employment issues. This not only concerns the relationship between welfare reform and labour market policy as they affect older people. Issues around health and education should also be considered. There is also the need to take account of wider equality and diversity issues and how public policies can be better integrated so as to properly reflect the needs of business" (Taylor, 2002, p. 15). Moreover, older worker's issues should be placed within a broader equality and diversity framework, oriented at age diversity and the life-course perspective, to avoid their consideration as a separate issue. That concept refers to a lifecycle approach to labour market participation, both men and women, in order to identify the underlying trends, recognise the changing needs of people as they age, with a special reference made to groups with specific labour market difficulties.

Discussions on older workers in the labour market and policies aimed to keep them in employment as long as possible could be placed within a broad multidimensional topic of active ageing, extensively studied by Avramov and Mašková (2002). They point to social and economic resources of today's and tomorrow's elderly. They are healthier, wealthier, better educated, have greater social capital and more years ahead of them than previous generations. To leave them inactive means also a gross loss of their human and social capital. Therefore, policies towards active ageing should be considered in terms of reducing existing under-utilisation of productive capacity of older people as well.

An integrated approach towards pension, social welfare and employment policy would entail a co-ordinated set of public policies (education, health, safety and social protection, and employment) and would involve all relevant stakeholders. Stimulating and supporting them towards the effective management of age would require the reinforcement of the mediating role of the state rather than the disengagement of public authorities (see also Avramov and Mašková, 2002).

The barriers older workers face in the labour market result from the complex interactions between economic, psychological, social and institutional factors. More research is needed to identify these relationships and policy impacts. That field in transition countries is completely under-researched. Policies affecting older workers have been introduced recently. Their effects should be carefully studied, especially in the cross-country comparative perspective.

Bibliography

Avramov, D. and M. Mašková. 2002. *Active ageing in Europe.* Council of Europe.

Augusztinovics, M. 1999. "Pension systems and reforms in the transition countries", *Economic survey of Europe,* Economic Commission for Europe and United Nations, vol.3.

Atkinson, A.B. 1995. "The welfare state and economic performance". *Welfare state programme discussion paper WSP/109.* London School of Economics.

Blöndal, S. and S. Scarpetta. 1999a. "The retirement decisions in OECD countries". *Economics department working paper no. 202,* OECD. Paris.

Blöndal, S. and S. Scarpetta. 1999b. "Early retirement in OECD countries: the role of social security systems". *OECD Economic studies no. 29,* 1997/II. Paris.

Boroń, M. 2002. "Changes in labour force participation in Poland in the years 1992-2000 from the perspective of quality adjustments". *Studia Demograficzne 2: 28-45.*

Chłoń, A., Góra M. and M. Rutkowski. 1999. "Shaping pension reform in Poland: security through diversity". *Pension primer series, social protection discussion paper,* World Bank, Washington, D.C.

Commission européenne. 2001. "La protection sociale dans les états membres de l'UE et de l'Espace économique européen: situation au 1er janvier 2001 et évolution". *MISSOC.*

Disney, R.F. 1999. "Notional accounts as pension reform strategy: an evaluation". *Pension primer series,* World Bank, Washington, D.C.

Disney, R.F. and E.R. Whitehouse. 1999a. "Retirement: the demand side". *Social protection discussion paper.* World Bank, Washington, D.C.

Disney, R.F. and E.R. Whitehouse. 1999b. "Notional accounts pensions: microeconomic and macroeconomic aspects". *Social protection discussion paper.* World Bank, Washington, D.C.

Disney, R.F. and E.R. Whitehouse. 1999c. "Pensions plans and retirement incentives". *Social protection discussion paper.* World Bank, Washington, D.C.

Eurostat. 1999. *Central European countries' employment and labour market review,* no.1.

Eurostat. 2001. "Theme 1-2/ 2001, Regional labour force in the EU: recent patterns and future perspectives". *Statistics in focus, general statistics*

Fultz, E., and M. Ruck. 2001. *Pension reform in central and eastern Europe: an update on the restructuring of national pension schemes in selected countries,* International Labour Office, central and eastern European team, Budapest.

Gruber, J. and D.A. Wise. 1999. *Social security programs and retirement around the world.* University of Chicago Press for National Bureau of Economic Research.

Henkens, K. and H.P. Van Dalen. "Early retirement systems and behavior in an international perspective". In: Adams, G.A., and T.A. Beehr. *Retirement research: Current perspectives and future directions.* Forthcoming. New York: Springer.

Kalisch, D.W. and T. Aman. 1998. "Retirement income systems: the reform process across OECD countries". *Ageing working papers No. 3.4.* OECD, Paris.

Kapteyn, A. and K. de Vos. 1998. "Social security and labour force participation in the Netherlands". *American Economic Review,* 88: pp. 164-167.

Kerkhofs, M., Lindeboom, M. and J. Theeuwes. 1999. "Retirement, financial incentives and health". *Labour Economics* 6: 203-227.

Kinsella, K, and V.A. Velkoff. 2001. "An aging world: 2001", *International population reports,* November 2001, U.S. Department of Health and Human Services, National Institute on Aging, and U.S. Department of Commerce, U.S. Census Bureau.

Mašková, M. 2002. "Demography of ageing: between country similarities and differences", in: D. Avramov, and M. Mašková. *Active ageing in Europe.* Council of Europe.

OECD. 1995a. "The transition from work to retirement". *Social policy studies no.16,* Paris.

OECD. 1995b. "The labour market and older workers". *Social policy studies no.17,* Paris.

OECD. 1996. *Ageing in OECD countries.* Paris.

OECD. 1998a. "Work-force ageing in OECD countries", pp.123-151 in *Employment outlook,* Paris. (also Ageing working paper no.4.1.)

OECD.1998b. *Employment outlook,* Paris.

OECD. 2001a. *Employment outlook,* Paris.

OECD. 2001b. *Ageing and Income – Financial resources and retirement in 9 OECD countries.* Paris.

Pearce, D.L. and Punch A. "Europe's population and labour market beyond 2000, introduction and summary". In: Punch A., and D.L.Pearce (eds). 2000, *Europe's population and labour market beyond 2000.* Council of Europe.

Rutkowski, M. 1998. "A new generation of pension reform conquers the east – a taxonomy in transition economies". *Transition 4:16-19.*

Rutkowski, M. 2002a. "Strategic choices in pension reform in central and eastern Europe and Central Asia", paper presented at the *World Bank seminar,* Białobrzegi, Poland, March 2002.

Rutkowski, M. 2002b. "The future of pensions in Europe: paradigmatic and parametric reforms in EU accession countries in the context of EU pension systems changes", paper presented at the second thematic NIEPS workshop on: *Ageing, intergenerational solidarity and age-specific vulnerabilities,* The Hague, September 27-28, 2002.

Van Dalen, H.P. and K.Henkens. 2002. "Early retirement reform: can it and will it work". *Ageing and Society* 22: 209-231.

Vlasblom, J.D. and G.Nekkers. 2001. "Regional differences in labour force activity rates of persons aged 55+ within European Union". *Eurostat working papers: population and social conditions* 3/2001/E/no.6.

Taylor, P. 2001. "Comparative policy approaches towards older workers", report for *Scottish Enterprise,* Open Business School.

Taylor, P. 2002. "European Union policy for older workers", paper presented at the second thematic NIEPS workshop on: *Ageing, intergenerational solidarity and age-specific vulnerabilities,* The Hague, September 27-28, 2002.

World Bank. *Averting the old age crisis. Policies to protect the old and promote growth.* Oxford University Press, New York 1994.

Data sources

Council of Europe. 2001. *Recent demographic developments in Europe.* Strasbourg: Council of Europe Publishing.

Eurostat. 1995. *The European Union labour source survey.*

Eurostat. 2001. *Labour force survey 2000.*

Eurostat. *Central European countries employment and labour market review, studies and research,* different issues.

ILO. December 1996. *Economically active population 1950-2010,* Geneva.

ILO. Yearbook of Labour Statistics 2001, Geneva 2001.

OECD. 1998. *Labour Force Statistics, 1976-1996.* Paris.

United Nations. *World population prospects. The 2000 Revision.* Vol.II: Sex and age distribution of the world population. New York, 2001.

Appendix: tables

Table 1 – Working-age population in selected countries of Europe, 2001

Country	Population aged 15-64 1 January 2001 (thousands)	15-24	25-44	45-54	55-64	Share of working-age population	Age structure 15-24	25-44	45-54	55-64
TOTAL	336801.2	65463.5	150046.5	67264.7	54026.5	67.26	19.44	44.55	19.97	16.04
"Western" Europe	260086.3	47740.5	117945.1	51408.0	42992.8	66.87	18.36	45.35	19.77	16.53
Northern Europe	15673.7	2830.6	6758.2	3424.3	2660.7	65.54	18.06	43.12	21.85	16.98
Denmark	3562.9	605.4	1576.7	757.1	623.7	66.61	16.99	44.25	21.25	17.51
Finland	3467.6	659.0	1414.0	827.6	567.0	66.93	19.00	40.78	23.87	16.35
Norway	2922.2	540.9	1330.9	614.0	436.3	64.89	18.51	45.55	21.01	14.93
Sweden	5721.1	1025.3	2436.6	1225.5	1033.7	64.41	17.92	42.59	21.42	18.07
Central-western Europe	66273.1	10950.7	30350.5	12308.0	12663.9	67.98	16.52	45.80	18.57	19.11
Austria	5510.3	957.6	2602.3	1037.2	913.2	67.85	17.38	47.23	18.82	16.57
Germany *	55915.2	9159.5	25524.9	10276.0	10954.8	68.05	16.38	45.65	18.38	19.59
- FRG before unification *	45214.0	7159.7	20951.3	8330.4	8772.7	67.54	15.84	46.34	18.42	19.40
- Former GDR *	10701.2	1999.8	4573.6	1945.7	2182.1	70.32	18.69	42.74	18.18	20.39
Switzerland	4847.6	833.6	2223.4	994.7	795.9	67.29	17.20	45.87	20.52	16.42
North-western Europe	97606.8	18743.8	43896.0	20373.0	14594.1	65.62	19.20	44.97	20.87	14.95
Belgium *	6719.2	1243.9	3047.7	1387.1	1040.4	65.62	18.51	45.36	20.64	15.48
France	38420.4	7660.9	16906.6	8369.9	5483.0	65.08	19.94	44.00	21.78	14.27
Ireland *	2527.5	659.5	1089.9	458.9	319.2	66.93	26.09	43.12	18.16	12.63
Netherlands	10835.0	1893.2	4999.7	2324.4	1617.7	67.77	17.47	46.14	21.45	14.93
United Kingdom	39104.8	7286.3	17852.0	7832.7	6133.7	65.49	18.63	45.65	20.03	15.69
Southern Europe	80532.7	15215.4	36940.3	15302.7	13074.1	67.79	18.89	45.87	19.00	16.23
Greece	7123.4	1474.0	3109.9	1338.7	1200.8	67.57	20.69	43.66	18.79	16.86
Italy	38974.2	6605.9	17867.7	7741.4	6759.3	67.38	16.95	45.84	19.86	17.34
Portugal	6988.5	1468.4	3115.6	1305.9	1098.5	67.91	21.01	44.58	18.69	15.72
Spain	27446.6	5667.1	12847.2	4916.8	4015.5	68.41	20.65	46.81	17.91	14.63

Country	Population aged 15-64 1 January 2001 (thousands)	15-24	25-44	45-54	55-64	Share of working-age population	age structure			
							15-24	25-44	45-54	55-64
Central and eastern Europe	**76714,9**	**17723,0**	**32101,5**	**15856,7**	**11033,7**	**68.63**	**23.10**	**41.85**	**20.67**	**14.38**
Central Europe	*65326,7*	*15280,9*	*27141,5*	*13728,6*	*9175,6*	*68.81*	*23.39*	*41.55*	*21.02*	*14.05*
Bulgaria	5551,8	1170,6	2277,9	1178,4	924,9	68.12	21.09	41.03	21.23	16.66
Czech Republic	7179,1	1534,9	2929,0	1607,3	1108,0	69.93	21.38	40.80	22.39	15.43
Hungary *	6858,2	1507,3	2785,7	1459,3	1105,9	68.29	21.98	40.62	21.28	16.13
Poland	26625,1	6566,8	10998,7	5757,9	3301,8	68.90	24.66	41.31	21.63	12.40
Romania	15365,9	3584,4	6548,1	2971,8	2261,5	68.50	23.33	42.61	19.34	14.72
Slovak Republic	3746,5	916,9	1602,1	754,0	473,5	69.35	24.47	42.76	20.12	12.64
Baltic countries	*4996,5*	*1076,8*	*2177,2*	*917,8*	*824,6*	*67.29*	*21.55*	*43.57*	*18.37*	*16.50*
Estonia	916,6	200,3	378,1	184,4	153,9	67.07	21.85	41.25	20.12	16.78
Latvia	1596,7	342,0	671,4	300,9	282,5	67.48	21.42	42.05	18.84	17.69
Lithuania	2483,1	534,6	1127,7	432,5	388,3	67.24	21.53	45.42	17.42	15.64
other										
Slovenia	1395,3	288,5	605,6	292,4	208,8	70.11	20.68	43.40	20.96	14.96

* - data from 2000.
Source: Council of Europe, 2001, own calculations.

Table 1a – Working-age population in selected countries of Europe, 2001, males

Country	Population aged 15-64 1 January 2001 (thousands)	15-24	25-44	45-54	55-64	Share of working-age population	age structure			
							15-24	25-44	45-54	55-64
TOTAL	**168832,4**	**33421,7**	**75927,4**	**33395,3**	**26088,0**	**69.15**	**19.80**	**44.97**	**19.78**	**15.45**
"Western" Europe	**130866,8**	**24383,2**	**59746,7**	**25681,8**	**21055,2**	**68.82**	**18.63**	**45.65**	**19.62**	**16.09**
Northern Europe	7947,2	1445,1	3444,8	1732,8	1324,6	67.36	18.18	43.35	21.80	16.67
Denmark	1802,8	307,6	802,1	382,4	310,6	68.18	17.06	44.49	21.21	17.23
Finland	1752,1	336,7	720,6	417,7	277,1	69.27	19.22	41.13	23.84	15.82
Norway	1485,8	276,1	678,6	313,3	217,9	66.59	18.58	45.67	21.08	14.66
Sweden	2906,5	524,7	1243,5	619,4	518,9	66.17	18.05	42.78	21.31	17.85
Central-western Europe	33597,9	5599,5	15547,8	6198,5	6252,2	70.65	16.67	46.28	18.45	18.61
Austria	2774,3	487,5	1319,9	522,0	445,0	70.27	17.57	47.57	18.81	16.04
Germany *	28396,2	4687,5	13115,9	5177,3	5415,5	70.83	16.51	46.19	18.23	19.07
- FRG before unification *	22908,5	3635,8	10723,9	4189,5	4359,4	70.16	15.87	46.81	18.29	19.03
- Former GDR *	5487,7	1051,7	2392,1	987,8	1056,1	73.78	19.16	43.59	18.00	19.25
Switzerland	2427,4	424,4	1112,0	499,2	391,8	68.97	17.48	45.81	20.57	16.14
North-western Europe	49048,0	9563,6	22126,4	10172,4	7185,6	67.28	19.50	45.11	20.74	14.65
Belgium *	3383,6	631,7	1543,1	699,6	509,2	67.59	18.67	45.61	20.68	15.05
France	19130,4	3891,6	8401,2	4153,6	2684,0	66.71	20.34	43.92	21.71	14.03
Ireland *	1268,7	335,3	542,4	230,7	160,3	67.65	26.43	42.75	18.18	12.64
Netherlands	5493,5	963,3	2538,9	1178,9	812,4	69.45	17.54	46.22	21.46	14.79
United Kingdom	19771,8	3741,7	9100,8	3909,6	3019,7	67.17	18.92	46.03	19.77	15.27
Southern Europe	40273,7	7775,0	18627,8	7578,1	6292,8	69.56	19.31	46.25	18.82	15.63
Greece	3561,8	755,0	1559,3	667,9	579,6	68.56	21.20	43.78	18.75	16.27
Italy	19506,2	3375,2	9022,4	3843,4	3265,3	69.43	17.30	46.25	19.70	16.74
Portugal	3437,6	744,9	1547,6	632,0	513,1	69.23	21.67	45.02	18.39	14.93
Spain	13768,2	2900,0	6498,5	2434,9	1934,7	70.10	21.06	47.20	17.68	14.05

Country	Population aged 15-64 1 January 2001 (thousands)	15-24	25-44	45-54	55-64	Share of working-age population	age structure			
							15-24	25-44	45-54	55-64
Central and eastern Europe	**37965,5**	**9038,5**	**16180,7**	**7713,5**	**5032,8**	**70.29**	**23.81**	**42.62**	**20.32**	**13.26**
Central Europe	*32443,0*	*7795,7*	*13712,7*	*6711,8*	*4222,8*	*70.35*	*24.03*	*42.27*	*20.69*	*13.02*
Bulgaria	2751,2	600,5	1146,2	572,1	432,4	69.34	21.83	41.66	20.79	15.72
Czech Republic	3595,0	784,1	1490,1	796,4	524,3	71.95	21.81	41.45	22.15	14.58
Hungary *	3367,3	770,5	1403,2	703,1	490,5	70.27	22.88	41.67	20.88	14.57
Poland	13233,3	3344,4	5558,1	2817,1	1513,8	70.49	25.27	42.00	21.29	11.44
Romania	7636,0	1828,6	3305,4	1453,3	1048,8	69.65	23.95	43.29	19.03	13.74
Slovak Republic	1860,1	467,6	809,6	369,9	213,0	70.83	25.14	43.52	19.89	11.45
Baltic countries	*2407,1*	*547,1*	*1079,7*	*425,6*	*354,7*	*69.56*	*22.73*	*44.85*	*17.68*	*14.73*
Estonia	437,7	102,0	184,7	85,0	66,0	69.43	23.31	42.19	19.42	15.08
Latvia	764,9	174,2	330,7	139,2	120,8	70.21	22.78	43.24	18.19	15.79
Lithuania	1204,6	270,9	564,3	201,5	167,9	69.20	22.49	46.85	16.73	13.94
other										
Slovenia	708,3	148,5	308,7	150,4	100,7	72.81	20.97	43.58	21.24	14.21

* - data from 2000.
Source: Council of Europe, 2001, own calculations.

Table 1b – Working-age population in selected countries of Europe, 2001, females

Country	Population aged 15-64 1 January 2001 (thousands)	15-24	25-44	45-54	55-64	Share of working-age population	age structure 15-24	25-44	45-54	55-64
TOTAL	167968,9	32041,8	74119,1	33869,4	27938,5	65.47	19.08	44.13	20.16	16.63
"Western" Europe	129219,5	23357,3	58198,4	25726,2	21937,6	65.00	18.08	45.04	19.91	16.98
Northern Europe	7726,5	1385,5	3313,5	1691,4	1336,1	63.76	17.93	42.88	21.89	17.29
Denmark	1760,1	297,8	774,6	374,7	313,0	65.07	16.92	44.01	21.29	17.79
Finland	1715,4	322,3	693,4	409,9	289,9	64.69	18.79	40.42	23.89	16.90
Norway	1436,4	264,8	652,4	300,8	218,5	63.22	18.43	45.42	20.94	15.21
Sweden	2814,6	500,6	1193,1	606,2	514,7	62.69	17.79	42.39	21.54	18.29
Central-western Europe	32675,2	5351,2	14802,7	6109,5	6411,7	65.44	16.38	45.30	18.70	19.62
Austria	2736,0	470,0	1282,4	515,3	468,2	65.55	17.18	46.87	18.83	17.11
Germany *	27519,0	4472,0	12409,0	5098,7	5539,3	65.41	16.25	45.09	18.53	20.13
- FRG before unification *	22305,5	3523,9	10227,4	4140,9	4413,3	65.04	15.80	45.85	18.56	19.79
- Former GDR *	5213,5	948,1	2181,6	957,9	1126,0	67.01	18.19	41.84	18.37	21.60
Switzerland	2420,2	409,2	1111,4	495,5	404,2	65.69	16.91	45.92	20.47	16.70
North-western Europe	48558,8	9180,1	21769,6	10200,6	7408,4	64.02	18.97	44.83	21.01	15.26
Belgium *	3335,6	612,3	1504,6	687,5	531,2	63.74	18.36	45.11	20.61	15.93
France	19290,0	3769,3	8505,4	4216,2	2799,0	63.53	19.54	44.09	21.86	14.51
Ireland *	1258,8	324,1	547,6	228,2	158,9	66.21	25.75	43.50	18.13	12.62
Netherlands	5341,5	929,9	2460,8	1145,5	805,3	66.13	17.41	46.07	21.45	15.08
United Kingdom	19333,0	3544,6	8751,2	3923,2	3114,0	63.86	18.33	45.27	20.29	16.11
Southern Europe	40258,9	7440,4	18312,5	7724,6	6781,3	66.10	18.48	45.49	19.19	16.84
Greece	3561,6	719,0	1550,6	670,8	621,1	66.60	20.19	43.54	18.84	17.44
Italy	19468,0	3230,7	8845,3	3898,0	3494,0	65.44	16.59	45.44	20.02	17.95
Portugal	3550,9	723,6	1568,0	673,9	585,4	66.68	20.38	44.16	18.98	16.49
Spain	13678,4	2767,1	6348,6	2481,9	2080,8	66.78	20.23	46.41	18.14	15.21

Country	Population aged 15-64 1 January 2001 (thousands)	15-24	25-44	45-54	55-64	Share of working-age population	age structure			
							15-24	25-44	45-54	55-64
Central and eastern Europe	**38749,4**	**8684,5**	**15920,7**	**8143,2**	**6000,9**	**67.08**	**22.41**	**41.09**	**21.01**	**15.49**
Central Europe	*32883,7*	*7485,2*	*13428,8*	*7016,8*	*4952,8*	*67.36*	*22.76*	*40.84*	*21.34*	*15.06*
Bulgaria	2800,6	570,2	1131,6	606,3	492,4	66.97	20.36	40.41	21.65	17.58
Czech Republic	3584,1	750,8	1438,8	810,9	583,7	68.01	20.95	40.14	22.62	16.28
Hungary *	3490,8	736,7	1382,4	756,2	615,5	66.47	21.11	39.60	21.66	17.63
Poland	13391,8	3222,4	5440,6	2940,8	1788,0	67.39	24.06	40.63	21.96	13.35
Romania	7729,9	1755,9	3242,8	1518,6	1212,7	67.41	22.72	41.95	19.65	15.69
Slovak Republic	1886,4	449,3	792,6	384,1	260,5	67.94	23.82	42.01	20.36	13.81
Baltic countries	*2589,4*	*529,7*	*1097,5*	*492,2*	*470,0*	*65.31*	*20.46*	*42.39*	*19.01*	*18.15*
Estonia	479,0	98,3	193,4	99,5	87,8	65.05	20.51	40.38	20.76	18.34
Latvia	831,8	167,7	340,7	161,7	161,8	65.16	20.16	40.95	19.44	19.45
Lithuania	1278,6	263,7	563,4	231,1	220,4	65.50	20.62	44.07	18.07	17.24
other										
Slovenia	687,0	140,0	296,9	142,0	108,1	67.53	20.38	43.22	20.67	15.74

* - data from 2000.
Source: Council of Europe, 2001, own calculations.

Table 2 – Life expectancy at selected ages

Country	e(0)				e(45)				e(65)			
	Males		Females		Males		Females		Males		Females	
	1990	2000	1990	2000	1990	2000	1990	2000	1990	2000	1990	2000
"Western" Europe												
Northern Europe												
Denmark	72.05	74.48	77.81	79.26	29.73	31.59	34.48	35.53	13.98	15.17	17.86	18.35
Finland	70.99	74.18	78.86	80.96	29.12	31.59	35.46	37.26	13.71	15.45	17.63	19.29
Norway	73.50	75.96	79.77	81.41	31.05	33.18	36.28	37.60	14.59	16.04	18.48	19.69
Sweden	74.82	77.38	80.37	81.73	32.00	33.98	36.79	37.72	15.27	16.66	18.97	19.84
Central-western Europe												
Austria	72.35	75.45	78.81	81.20	30.20	32.66	35.48	37.48	14.39	16.23	17.83	19.56
Germany 1999	71.95	74.74	78.37	80.74	29.69	31.86	35.06	37.02	13.96	15.48	17.52	19.16
- FRG before unification 1997	72.67	74.41	78.97	80.46	30.20	31.55	35.59	36.79	14.24	15.26	17.92	19.01
- Former GDR 1997	69.21	72.41	76.20	79.48	27.65	30.18	33.13	35.89	12.77	14.43	15.98	18.12
Switzerland	74.00	76.93	80.72	82.59	31.90	34.04	37.36	38.79	15.27	16.94	19.38	20.67
North-western Europe												
Belgium 1999	72.71	74.38	79.33	80.82	30.45	31.73	36.09	37.20	14.23	15.37	18.44	19.41
France 1998	72.75	74.78	80.88	82.40	31.08	32.36	37.67	38.84	15.54	16.38	19.84	20.89
Ireland	72.11	74.22	77.67	79.17	29.51	31.41	34.24	35.48	13.30	14.57	16.92	17.71
Netherlands	73.83	75.51	80.04	80.54	30.95	32.27	36.60	36.88	14.38	15.28	18.89	19.17
United Kingdom	72.89	75.44	78.55	80.18	30.29	32.48	35.14	36.53	14.02	15.64	17.90	18.87

Southern Europe												
Greece 1999	74.63	75.45	79.35	80.62	32.36	32.95	36.08	36.98	15.64	16.30	17.86	18.66
Italy 1998	73.64	75.74	80.09	81.76	31.37	32.90	36.66	38.06	15.04	16.00	18.71	19.91
Portugal	70.44	72.72	77.28	79.68	29.67	31.03	34.59	36.29	13.91	14.74	16.91	18.29
Spain	73.34	75.45	80.30	82.71	31.66	33.01	37.07	39.01	15.44	16.40	18.96	20.56
Central and eastern Europe												
Central Europe												
Bulgaria	67.96	68.49	74.67	75.08	27.26	27.07	32.28	32.48	12.69	12.78	15.12	15.33
Czech Republic	67.62	71.67	75.45	78.38	25.86	28.93	32.34	34.62	11.66	13.72	15.27	17.11
Hungary	65.16	67.18	73.72	75.71	24.83	25.59	31.56	32.76	12.00	12.57	15.27	16.31
Poland	66.50	69.72	75.50	77.91	26.00	27.90	33.00	34.55	12.40	13.59	16.10	17.35
Romania	66.59	67.73	73.04	74.64	27.30	27.29	31.89	32.61	13.11	13.37	15.07	15.75
Slovak Republic	66.66	69.18	75.53	77.41	25.48	27.16	32.65	33.94	12.22	12.93	15.79	16.55
Baltic countries												
Estonia	64.78	65.61	74.96	76.37	25.26	25.25	32.54	33.55	12.03	12.65	15.67	16.90
Latvia	64.26	65.01	74.56	76.09	25.11	25.19	32.38	33.52	12.05	12.59	15.78	16.90
Lithuania	66.54	67.54	76.30	77.69	26.63	27.15	33.82	34.92	13.35	13.87	16.99	17.90
other												
Slovenia	69.84	72.27	77.80	79.72	27.90	29.64	34.42	36.08	13.28	14.17	16.94	18.52

Source: Recent demographic developments in Europe 2001. Council of Europe. 2002.

Table 3 – Projections of the working-age population in selected countries of Europe, 2001

year	UN projections. Medium variant										
	2000	2005	2010	2015	2020	2025	2030	2035	2040	2045	2050
TOTAL	330880	332480	332544	326081	316735	304504	289945	275391	262957	252320	242539
"Western" Europe	259405	260115	260215	256046	250015	240910	228633	216746	207812	201357	195240
Northern Europe	15607	15868	15975	15598	15166	14652	14070	13555	13230	13031	12823
Denmark	3551	3566	3563	3513	3459	3366	3231	3103	3016	2988	2997
Finland	3466	3492	3504	3369	3226	3092	2968	2879	2838	2766	2678
Norway	2897	3004	3081	3083	3057	2995	2920	2841	2800	2809	2819
Sweden	5693	5806	5827	5633	5424	5199	4951	4732	4576	4468	4329
Central-western Europe	66134	65307	64596	63901	61846	58775	54744	51233	49605	48405	46736
Austria	5481	5485	5447	5353	5176	4874	4479	4109	3874	3714	3512
Germany	55824	55002	54404	53964	52304	49830	46525	43635	42381	41441	40106
Switzerland	4829	4820	4745	4584	4366	4071	3740	3489	3350	3250	3118
North-western Europe	97546	99734	101379	100350	99105	96980	93943	91286	89496	88657	87346
Belgium	6734	6803	6900	6800	6621	6360	6071	5848	5689	5569	5439
France	38678	39512	40135	39625	39088	38469	37699	36980	36251	35884	35412
Ireland	2553	2706	2806	2869	2950	3045	3132	3207	3223	3182	3163
Netherlands	10796	11034	11211	11080	10897	10567	10120	9697	9466	9403	9323
United Kingdom	38785	39679	40327	39976	39549	38539	36921	35554	34867	34619	34009
Southern Europe	80118	79206	78265	76197	73898	70503	65876	60672	55481	51264	48335
Greece	7150	7099	7047	6919	6727	6459	6142	5766	5385	5023	4738
Italy	38916	38093	37454	36196	34941	33172	30678	27985	25527	23824	22630
Portugal	6782	6753	6745	6688	6597	6434	6201	5906	5539	5217	5024
Spain	27270	27261	27019	26394	25633	24438	22855	21015	19030	17200	15943

Central and eastern Europe	71475	72365	72329	70035	66720	63594	61312	58645	55145	50963	47299
Central Europe	*65007*	*65881*	*65917*	*63830*	*60815*	*58035*	*56107*	*53746*	*50565*	*46702*	*43381*
Bulgaria	5414	5301	5115	4765	4429	4111	3812	3521	3187	2835	2540
Czech Republic	7164	7272	7203	6867	6548	6300	6045	5766	5323	4844	4530
Hungary	6818	6745	6641	6412	6049	5756	5552	5281	4916	4501	4238
Poland	26525	27202	27634	26870	25525	24254	23507	22900	21850	20390	18805
Romania	15356	15497	15397	15048	14533	14018	13714	12917	12118	11201	10558
Slovak Republic	3730	3864	3927	3868	3731	3596	3477	3361	3171	2931	2710
Baltic countries	*5073*	*5086*	*5030*	*4866*	*4642*	*4372*	*4095*	*3864*	*3617*	*3381*	*3112*
Estonia	946	917	884	825	764	704	649	597	542	487	431
Latvia	1644	1643	1617	1549	1472	1385	1302	1233	1157	1081	991
Lithuania	2483	2526	2529	2492	2406	2283	2144	2034	1918	1813	1690
other											
Slovenia	1395	1398	1382	1339	1263	1187	1110	1035	963	880	806

Source: World population prospects. The 2000 revision. Vol.II: Sex and age distribution of the world population. United Nations. New York, 2001.

Table 4 – Absolute changes in the working-age population in selected countries of Europe (t/t-1)

	2005	2010	2015	2020	2025	2030	2035	2040	2045	2050	2050
TOTAL	1600	64	-6463	-9346	-12231	-14559	-14554	-12434	-10637	-9781	242539
"Western" Europe	710	100	-4169	-6031	-9105	-12277	-11887	-8934	-6455	-6117	195240
Northern Europe	*261*	*107*	*-377*	*-432*	*-514*	*-582*	*-515*	*-325*	*-199*	*-208*	*12823*
Denmark	15	-3	-50	-54	-93	-135	-128	-87	-28	9	2997
Finland	26	12	-135	-143	-134	-124	-89	-41	-72	-88	2678
Norway	107	77	2	-26	-62	-75	-79	-41	9	10	2819
Sweden	113	21	-194	-209	-225	-248	-219	-156	-108	-139	4329
Central-western Europe	*-827*	*-711*	*-695*	*-2055*	*-3071*	*-4031*	*-3511*	*-1628*	*-1200*	*-1669*	*46736*
Austria	4	-38	-94	-177	-302	-395	-370	-235	-160	-202	3512
Germany	-822	-598	-440	-1660	-2474	-3305	-2890	-1254	-940	-1335	40106
Switzerland	-9	-75	-161	-218	-295	-331	-251	-139	-100	-132	3118
North-western Europe	*2188*	*1645*	*-1029*	*-1245*	*-2125*	*-3037*	*-2657*	*-1790*	*-839*	*-1311*	*87346*
Belgium	69	97	-100	-179	-261	-289	-223	-159	-120	-130	5439
France	834	623	-510	-537	-619	-770	-719	-729	-367	-472	35412
Ireland	153	100	63	81	95	87	75	16	-41	-19	3163
Netherlands	238	177	-131	-183	-330	-447	-423	-231	-63	-80	9323
United Kingdom	894	648	-351	-427	-1010	-1618	-1367	-687	-248	-610	34009
Southern Europe	*-912*	*-941*	*-2068*	*-2299*	*-3395*	*-4627*	*-5204*	*-5191*	*-4217*	*-2929*	*48335*
Greece	-51	-52	-128	-192	-268	-317	-376	-381	-362	-285	4738
Italy	-823	-639	-1258	-1255	-1769	-2494	-2693	-2458	-1703	-1194	22630
Portugal	-29	-8	-57	-91	-163	-233	-295	-367	-322	-193	5024
Spain	-9	-242	-625	-761	-1195	-1583	-1840	-1985	-1830	-1257	15943

Central and eastern Europe	890	-36	-2294	-3315	-3126	-2282	-2667	-3500	-4182	-3664	47299
Central Europe	*874*	*36*	*-2087*	*-3015*	*-2780*	*-1928*	*-2361*	*-3181*	*-3863*	*-3321*	*43381*
Bulgaria	-113	-186	-350	-336	-318	-299	-291	-334	-352	-295	2540
Czech Republic	108	-69	-336	-319	-248	-255	-279	-443	-479	-314	4530
Hungary	-73	-104	-229	-363	-293	-204	-271	-365	-415	-263	4238
Poland	677	432	-764	-1345	-1271	-747	-607	-1050	-1460	-1585	18805
Romania	141	-100	-349	-515	-515	-304	-797	-799	-917	-643	10558
Slovak Republic	134	63	-59	-137	-135	-119	-116	-190	-240	-221	2710
Baltic countries	*13*	*-56*	*-164*	*-224*	*-270*	*-277*	*-231*	*-247*	*-236*	*-269*	*3112*
Estonia	-29	-33	-59	-61	-60	-55	-52	-55	-55	-56	431
Latvia	-1	-26	-68	-77	-87	-83	-69	-76	-76	-90	991
Lithuania	43	3	-37	-86	-123	-139	-110	-116	-105	-123	1690
other											
Slovenia	3	-16	-43	-76	-76	-77	-75	-72	-83	-74	806

Source: Own calculations based on Table 2.

Table 5 – Projected size of the population aged 55-64

	2000	2005	2010	2015	2020	2025	2030	2035	2040	2045	2050
							UN projections. Medium variant				
TOTAL	53115	57118	62749	65842	69521	71571	69509	65311	62097	60213	57697
"Western" Europe	42881	45952	49450	51860	56640	59246	56190	50704	47357	46362	45452
Northern Europe	2613	3173	3327	3205	3285	3370	3251	2985	2798	2869	3094
Denmark	614	725	733	709	749	785	766	695	600	585	659
Finland	557	703	790	745	724	695	626	607	636	629	629
Norway	428	543	602	612	639	671	670	602	551	574	625
Sweden	1014	1202	1202	1139	1173	1219	1189	1081	1011	1081	1181
Central-western Europe	12548	11576	11986	13529	15284	15941	13712	11334	11124	11679	11503
Austria	913	961	970	1073	1253	1334	1195	977	913	925	923
Germany	10785	9654	10021	11415	12904	13505	11587	9579	9468	9981	9780
Switzerland	850	961	995	1041	1127	1102	930	778	743	773	800
North-western Europe	14618	17381	19504	19881	21332	21967	20960	19157	18486	19039	19100
Belgium	1047	1171	1340	1426	1515	1497	1393	1295	1249	1253	1266
France	5481	6690	7946	8056	8184	8184	8081	7673	7404	7474	7242
Ireland	327	394	451	483	508	517	558	649	699	654	582
Netherlands	1603	1975	2201	2251	2435	2548	2406	2088	1922	1980	2084
United Kingdom	6160	7151	7566	7665	8690	9221	8522	7452	7212	7678	7926
Southern Europe	13102	13822	14633	15245	16739	17968	18267	17228	14949	12775	11755
Greece	1213	1228	1319	1396	1469	1550	1595	1575	1480	1294	1140
Italy	6799	7089	7398	7488	8278	8938	8834	7845	6551	5799	5575
Portugal	1063	1118	1205	1262	1328	1399	1513	1553	1397	1176	1087
Spain	4027	4387	4711	5099	5664	6081	6325	6255	5521	4506	3953

Central and eastern Europe	10234	11166	13299	13982	12881	12325	13319	14607	14740	13851	12245
Central Europe	*9186*	*10153*	*12211*	*12788*	*11627*	*11094*	*12128*	*13432*	*13555*	*12632*	*11146*
Bulgaria	901	951	1002	954	901	868	895	950	911	823	716
Czech Republic	1094	1373	1504	1395	1290	1291	1461	1646	1513	1310	1216
Hungary	1100	1175	1315	1324	1135	1107	1276	1418	1304	1127	1087
Poland	3323	3886	5114	5604	5118	4455	4641	5345	5852	5612	4826
Romania	2296	2218	2598	2768	2463	2692	3133	3248	3128	2970	2586
Slovak Republic	472	550	678	743	720	681	722	825	847	790	715
Baltic countries	*834*	*784*	*817*	*901*	*965*	*949*	*917*	*896*	*909*	*968*	*883*
Estonia	154	143	155	159	154	144	140	138	138	141	117
Latvia	287	265	274	300	313	302	292	287	301	326	289
Lithuania	393	376	388	442	498	503	485	471	470	501	477
other											
Slovenia	214	229	271	293	289	282	274	279	276	251	216

Source: own calculations based on data from World population prospects. The 2000 Revision. Vol.II: Sex and age distribution of the world population. United Nations. New York, 2001.

Table 6 – Absolute changes in the population aged 55-64. Selected European countries (t/t-1)

	2005	2010	2015	2020	2025	2030	2035	2040	2045	2050
TOTAL	4003	5631	3093	3679	2050	-2062	-4198	-3214	-1884	-2516
"Western" Europe	3071	3498	2410	4780	2606	-3056	-5486	-3347	-995	-910
Northern Europe	*560*	*154*	*-122*	*80*	*85*	*-119*	*-266*	*-187*	*71*	*225*
Denmark	111	8	-24	40	36	-19	-71	-95	-15	74
Finland	146	87	-45	-21	-29	-69	-19	29	-7	0
Norway	115	59	10	27	32	-1	-68	-51	23	51
Sweden	188	0	-63	34	46	-30	-108	-70	70	100
Central-western Europe	*-972*	*410*	*1543*	*1755*	*657*	*-2229*	*-2378*	*-210*	*555*	*-176*
Austria	48	9	103	180	81	-139	-218	-64	12	-2
Germany	-1131	367	1394	1489	601	-1918	-2008	-111	513	-201
Switzerland	111	34	46	86	-25	-172	-152	-35	30	27
North-western Europe	*2763*	*2123*	*377*	*1451*	*635*	*-1007*	*-1803*	*-671*	*553*	*61*
Belgium	124	169	86	89	-18	-104	-98	-46	4	13
France	1209	1256	110	128	0	-103	-408	-269	70	-232
Ireland	67	57	32	25	9	41	91	50	-45	-72
Netherlands	372	226	50	184	113	-142	-318	-166	58	104
United Kingdom	991	415	99	1025	531	-699	-1070	-240	466	248
Southern Europe	*720*	*811*	*612*	*1494*	*1229*	*299*	*-1039*	*-2279*	*-2174*	*-1020*
Greece	15	91	77	73	81	45	-20	-95	-186	-154
Italy	290	309	90	790	660	-104	-989	-1294	-752	-224
Portugal	55	87	57	66	71	114	40	-156	-221	-89
Spain	360	324	388	565	417	244	-70	-734	-1015	-553

Central and eastern Europe	932	2133	683	-1101	-556	994	1288	133	-889	-1606
Central Europe	*967*	*2058*	*577*	*-1161*	*-533*	*1034*	*1304*	*123*	*-923*	*-1486*
Bulgaria	50	51	-48	-53	-33	27	55	-39	-88	-107
Czech Republic	279	131	-109	-105	1	170	185	-133	-203	-94
Hungary	75	140	9	-189	-28	169	142	-114	-177	-40
Poland	563	1228	490	-486	-663	186	704	507	-240	-786
Romania	-78	380	170	-305	229	441	115	-120	-158	-384
Slovak Republic	78	128	65	-23	-39	41	103	22	-57	-75
Baltic countries	*-50*	*33*	*84*	*64*	*-16*	*-32*	*-21*	*13*	*59*	*-85*
Estonia	-11	12	4	-5	-10	-4	-2	0	3	-24
Latvia	-22	9	26	13	-11	-10	-5	14	25	-37
Lithuania	-17	12	54	56	5	-18	-14	-1	31	-24
other										
Slovenia	15	42	22	-4	-7	-8	5	-3	-25	-35

Source: Own calculations based on Table 5.

Table 7 – Ageing of the working-age population, 2000-2050

	The share of persons aged 55-64 in the working-age population (percent)										
	2000	2005	2010	2015	2020	2025	2030	2035	2040	2045	2050
"Western" Europe											
Northern Europe											
Denmark	17.29	20.33	20.57	20.18	21.65	23.32	23.71	22.40	19.89	19.58	21.99
Finland	16.07	20.13	22.55	22.11	22.44	22.48	21.09	21.08	22.41	22.74	23.49
Norway	14.77	18.08	19.54	19.85	20.90	22.40	22.95	21.19	19.68	20.43	22.17
Sweden	17.81	20.70	20.63	20.22	21.63	23.45	24.02	22.84	22.09	24.19	27.28
Central-western Europe											
Austria	16.66	17.52	17.81	20.04	24.21	27.37	26.68	23.78	23.57	24.91	26.28
Germany	19.32	17.55	18.42	21.15	24.67	27.10	24.90	21.95	22.34	24.08	24.39
Switzerland	17.60	19.94	20.97	22.71	25.81	27.07	24.87	22.30	22.18	23.78	25.66
North-western Europe											
Belgium	15.55	17.21	19.42	20.97	22.88	23.54	22.95	22.14	21.95	22.50	23.28
France	14.17	16.93	19.80	20.33	20.94	21.27	21.44	20.75	20.42	20.83	20.45
Ireland	12.81	14.56	16.07	16.84	17.22	16.98	17.82	20.24	21.69	20.55	18.40
Netherlands	14.85	17.90	19.63	20.32	22.35	24.11	23.77	21.53	20.30	21.06	22.35
United Kingdom	15.88	18.02	18.76	19.17	21.97	23.93	23.08	20.96	20.68	22.18	23.31
Southern Europe											
Greece	16.97	17.30	18.72	20.18	21.84	24.00	25.97	27.32	27.48	25.76	24.06
Italy	17.47	18.61	19.75	20.69	23.69	26.94	28.80	28.03	25.66	24.34	24.64
Portugal	15.67	16.56	17.87	18.87	20.13	21.74	24.40	26.30	25.22	22.54	21.64
Spain	14.77	16.09	17.44	19.32	22.10	24.88	27.67	29.76	29.01	26.20	24.79

Central and eastern Europe											
Central Europe											
Bulgaria	16.64	17.94	19.59	20.02	20.34	21.11	23.48	26.98	28.58	29.03	28.19
Czech Republic	15.27	18.88	20.88	20.31	19.70	20.49	24.17	28.55	28.42	27.04	26.84
Hungary	16.13	17.42	19.80	20.65	18.76	19.23	22.98	26.85	26.53	25.04	25.65
Poland	12.53	14.29	18.51	20.86	20.05	18.37	19.74	23.34	26.78	27.52	25.66
Romania	14.95	14.31	16.87	18.39	16.95	19.20	22.85	25.15	25.81	26.52	24.49
Slovak Republic	12.65	14.23	17.27	19.21	19.30	18.94	20.77	24.55	26.71	26.95	26.38
Baltic countries											
Estonia	16.28	15.59	17.53	19.27	20.16	20.45	21.57	23.12	25.46	28.95	27.15
Latvia	17.46	16.13	16.94	19.37	21.26	21.81	22.43	23.28	26.02	30.16	29.16
Lithuania	15.83	14.89	15.34	17.74	20.70	22.03	22.62	23.16	24.50	27.63	28.22
other											
Slovenia	15.34	16.38	19.61	21.88	22.88	23.76	24.68	26.96	28.66	28.52	26.80

Source: own calculations based on data from World population prospects. The 2000 Revision. Vol.II: Sex and age distribution of the world population. United Nations. New York, 2001.

Table 8a – Labour force participation rates by age and sex: selected years 1970 to 1999, males

Country	Year	25-44	45-49	50-54	55-59	60-64	65+
Western Europe							
Austria	1971	97.1	95.8	92.7	83.7	44.9	8.0
	1981	96.5	96.3	91.5	77.3	23.3	3.1
	1988	95.0	94.7	90.0	65.3	14.2	1.8
	1996	93.6	94.3	86.6	63.7	16.7	4.6
Belgium	1970	96.2	92.2	89.2	82.3	79.3	6.8
	1981	94.5	90.8	85.7	70.7	32.3	3.3
	1999	94.7	91.1	80.3	52.4	18.6	2.8[1]
Denmark	1970	93.4	96.3	94.8	91.1	81.3	23.5
	1979	96.6	96.1	93.3	90.8	62	16.3
	1986	94.1	92.7	87.4	81.2	49.6	12.8
	1996	93.2	91.5	87.7	81.2	42	18.5[2]
France	1975	96.2	95.4	92.1	81.8	54.6	10.7
	1982	95.5	94.9	90.9	76.9	39.1	5.0
	1990	96.1	95.9	91.6	68.6	18.1	2.8
	1996	95.8	95	92.6	70.4	16.4	2.3
Germany	1970	96.7	95.9	93.2	86.8	68.8	16.0
	1980	96.1	96.8	93.3	82.3	44.2	7.4
	1988	94.1	96.4	93.2	79.8	34.5	4.9
	1999	93.8	94.5	90.5	76.5	30.3	4.5
Greece	1971	93.8	91.7[3]	...	75.3[4]	...	33.4
	1981	96.8	95.1	90.0	81.1	61.7	26.2
	1987	90.1	98.0	84.2	74.3	53.5	14.0
	1998	96.2	94.3	86.7	71.7	45.4	9.7
Italy	1971	95.5	92.1	87.2	75.0	40.6	13.4
	1981	96.2	93.2	85.7	65.1	29.1	6.9
	1989	95.6	95.6	87.5	67.8	35.2	7.9
	1998	91.7	93.5	80.1	54.1	31.7	6.3
Luxembourg	1970	98.0	95.9	91.4	79.3	45.5	10.1
	1981	97.4	96.0	90.0	54.3	28.0	6.5
	1996	95.7	95.0	84.0	52.7	16.7	2.5
	1999	95.1	94.7	87.1	53.4	15.5	1.9

Norway	1970	96.1[5]	95.7[6]	91.4[7]	...	73.6[8]	15.7[9]
	1980	94.3[5]	93.3[6]	87.7[7]	...	62.7[8]	12.6[9]
	1989	93.7	93.8	90.5	83.2	64.9	23.6
	1999	92.3	92.2	89.2	84.8	61.1	13.4[10]
Sweden	1970	90.0	92.9	91.9	88.4	75.7	15.2
	1980	90.6	92.0	89.8	84.4	65.9	8.1
	1985	90.6	92.1	90.3	85.3	63.2	11.3
	1999	88.7	90.7	89.2	84.4	55.5	...
United Kingdom	1971	98.0	98.1	97.1	95.1	86.4	19.4
	1981	97.5	97.3	95.7	91.5	74.6	10.7
	1986	93.9	91.6[3]	...	80.3	53.4	7.5
	1993	94.5	92.8	88.1	75.7	52.2	7.4
	1999	92.6[11]	...	44.7[12]	...	...	...
Central and eastern Europe							
Bulgaria	1975	96.8	95.7	92.0	86.5	33.6	10.3
	1985	96.4	94.6	88.1	80.9	39.2	15.2
	1992	94.4	91.9	84.6	58.0	11.1	4.5
Czech Republic	1970	98.3	96.0	93.2	85.0	33.3	14.6
	1980	98.2	96.0	92.7	84.2	46.3	19.5
	1991	97.9	95.5	91.5	80.0	28.4	11.6
	1999	96.5	94.9	90.1	77.1	27.5	7.2
Hungary	1970	98.1	95.4	91.8	84.4	43.7	16.7
	1980	97.7	92.9	86.2	72.2	13.2	4.0
	1996	90.0	83.1	70.0	46.1	9.2	4.3
	1999	88.0	81.2	72.5	45.9	10.6	3.8[10]
Poland	1970	96.6	95.1	94.0	90.9	83.0	56.4
	1978	96.1	92.1	87.1	81.5	62.4	34.9
	1996	92.9	85.1	76.8	55.2	33.4	15.3
Russian Federation	1989	97.3	95.8	91.7	79.3	35.4	14.2
	1992	92.1[11]	...	93.9	80.5	38.1	20.7[13]
	1999	91.0	88.6	85.3	65.2	29.2	6.4

1. Refers to ages 65 to 69 years. 2. Refers to ages 65 to 66 years. 3. Refers to ages 45 to 54 years. 4. Refers to ages 55 to 64 years. 5. Refers to ages 25 to 39 years. 6. Refers to ages 40 to 49 years. 7. Refers to ages 50 to 59 years. 8. Refers to ages 60 to 69 years. 9. Refers to ages 70 and over. 10. Refers to ages 65 to 74 years. 11. Refers to ages 25 to 49 years. 12. Refers to ages 50 years and over. 13. Refers to ages 65 to 72 years.

Source: K.Kinsella. and V. A.Velkoff., *An Aging World: 2001*. International population reports. November 2001. U.S. Department of Health and Human Services. National Institute on Aging. and U.S. Department of Commerce. U.S.Census Bureau.

Table 8b – Labour force participation rates by age and sex: selected years 1970 to 1999, females

Country	Year	25-44	45-49	50-54	55-59	60-64	65+
Western Europe							
Austria	1971	52.8	53.7	48.5	35.8	13.2	3.2
	1981	62.2	57.3	53.5	32.4	9.5	1.8
	1988	63.9	59.4	51.6	24.6	5.7	0.9
	1996	76.7	69.2	59.3	25.4	8.7	2.0
Belgium	1970	39.1	30.8	27.6	20.0	7.6	2.2
	1981	60.1	38.2	30.7	17.3	5.7	1.0
	1999	79.3	65.0	48.5	27.6	6.7	0.8[1]
Denmark	1970	55.5	54.4	49.5	39.8	24.9	4.6
	1979	84.2	76.1	66.9	54.8	32.5	4.3
	1986	87.9	81.9	72.9	60.5	26.6	3.3
	1996	84.7	82.3	72.7	58.7	20.5	8.7[2]
France	1975	55.0	49.4	48.2	42.1	27.9	5.0
	1982	66.6	58.3	54.1	45.0	22.3	2.2
	1990	77.2	71.8	63.2	46.8	16.7	1.5
	1996	81.3	80.9	71.5	51.7	15.2	2.0
Germany	1970	47.4	48.3	42.8	34.5	17.7	5.7
	1980	57.1	52.2	47.2	38.7	13.0	3.0
	1988	64.6	60.9	53.7	41.1	11.1	1.8
	1999	77.1	78.3	70.5	55.3	12.7	1.6
Greece	1971	30.9	27.9[3]	...	19.8[4]	...	8.4
	1981	33.4	28.9	25.8	20.0	13.4	5.0
	1987	52.2	43.9	37.2	29.3	22.0	5.1
	1998	66.2	51.7	40.4	28.1	21.2	3.6
Italy	1971	31.8	29.7	26.3	16.9	9.9	3.2
	1981	19.8	36.2	30.2	16.9	8.0	1.5
	1989	59.5	44.7	34.1	20.2	9.8	2.2
	1998	60.8	50.9	38.7	22.7	8.1	1.7
Luxembourg	1970	26.3	23.9	22.1	18.6	12.0	4.0
	1981	46.4	30.3	25.6	20.1	12.4	2.8
	1996	61.3	49.0	35.6	14.9	5.1	0.9
	1999	65.6	60.3	44.1	24.6	11.7	0.6

Norway	1970	42.9	48.7	46.8	...	26.0	3.7
	1980	67.8[5]	74.0[6]	61.0[7]	...	32.2[8]	2.9[9]
	1989	78.9	82.0	75.8	63.2	44.1	11.8
	1999	83.2	85.9	80.1	71.3	49.5	8.8[10]
Sweden	1970	49.6	55.0	50.3	41.1	25.7	3.2
	1980	77.0	82.9	77.8	66.4	41.4	2.6
	1985	85.6	87.5	83.1	72.5	45.6	3.1
	1999	83.4	88.1	85.6	79.0	46.5	...
United Kingdom	1971	50.4	61.3	58.9	50.7	27.8	6.4
	1981	59.4	68.5	63.5	52.0	22.5	3.7
	1986	66.9	69.9[3]	...	51.5	18.8	2.7
	1993	73.5	77.9	70.0	54.5	24.7	3.5
	1999	76.6[11]	...	28.2[12]	...	...	...
Central and eastern Europe							
Bulgaria	1975	92.7	86.4	75.4	26.1	8.2	1.7
	1985	95.3	91.0	83.6	32.0	16.5	4.3
	1992	93.7	92.9	75.5	10.7	4.7	2.1
Czech Republic	1970	79.7	77.3	70.1	36.5	18.2	5.2
	1980	91.8	88.1	79.9	40.8	21.5	6.5
	1991	95.1	93.4	85.7	31.1	16.2	4.9
	1999	79.9	90.8	81.5	33.2	12.9	2.7
Hungary	1970	68.6	64	56.6	29.2	17.1	5.8
	1980	79.2	77.5	67.4	18.8	8.7	2.9
	1996	69.8	76.1	55.4	15.5	6.0	2.1
	1999	70.4	75.3	61.9	16.6	5.5	1.6[10]
Poland	1970	78.3	79.2	75.9	68.1	51.1	33.0
	1978	79.2	78.5	71.6	57.9	37.4	19.4
	1996	79.5	79.1	63.1	35	19.2	8.5
Russian Federation	1989	93.8	93.7	83.8	34.8	20.4	6.4
	1992	88.9[10]	...	83.6	43.0	21.0	11.0[13]
	1999	84.4	86.8	78.9	33.7	16.0	2.5

1. Refers to ages 65 to 69 years. 2. Refers to ages 65 to 66 years. 3. Refers to ages 45 to 54 years. 4. Refers to ages 55 to 64 years. 5. Refers to ages 25 to 39 years. 6. Refers to ages 40 to 49 years. 7. Refers to ages 50 to 59 years. 8. Refers to ages 60 to 69 years. 9. Refers to ages 70 and over. 10. Refers to ages 65 to 74 years. 11. Refers to ages 25 to 49 years. 12. Refers to ages 50 years and over.13. Refers to ages 65 to 72 years.

Source: K.Kinsella. and V. A.Velkoff., *An aging world: 2001*. International population reports. November 2001. U.S. Department of Health and Human Services. National Institute on Aging. and U.S. Department of Commerce. U.S.Census Bureau.

Table 9 – Labour force participation rates of persons aged 55-69, 2000

Country	Males			Females		
	55-59	60-64	65-69	55-59	60-64	65-69
"Western" Europe						
Northern Europe						
Denmark	79.4	41.0	6.0	64.0	21.9	1.6
Finland	62.6	29.0	7.7	65.3	21.6	2.2
Norway	84.8	60.6	21.5	71.8	48.4	14.9
Sweden	89.9	83.8	56.2	85.7	79.4	48.2
Central-western Europe						
Austria	63.4	17.3	6.8	25.8	8.1	3.5
Germany	76.0	30.3	7.4	55.9	12.9	3.3
North-western Europe						
Belgium	56.5	18.5	2.5*	28.2	6.6	0.8*
France**	67.0	15.3	2.3˙	49.3	14.0	1.0˙
Netherlands	70.5	27.9	9.7	38.9	11.5	3.1
United Kingdom**	74.5	49.5	7.6˙	54.6	23.7	3.4˙
Southern Europe						
Greece	72.1	45.2	16.7	31.4	20.5	6.3
Italy	53.8	31.4	10.6	24.2	8.0	2.8
Portugal	73.8	55.8	33.7	47.8	36.7	21.0
Spain	75.6	5.5	1.1	28.5	16.6	2.5
Central and eastern Europe						
Central Europe						
Bulgaria	59.7	13.3	4.0	21.0	2.8	0.9
Czech Republic	75.0	23.4	6.6*	32.1	12.0	2.3*
Hungary	51.8	12.0	4.9	20.7	5.1	2.5
Poland	51.4	29.7	12.4*	31.7	16.3	5.2*
Romania	63.2	51.2	46.6	47.6	40.7	39.9
Slovak Republic	66.9	9.9	3.3	15.6	4.3	1.3
Baltic countries						
Estonia	75.9	48.5	22.1	52.0	25.9	15.8
Latvia	70.0	38.0	17.3	42.9	19.1	11.8
Lithuania	75.9	39.3	16.0	52.5	18.1	10.8

˙data for 65 and more.
**data for 1998 from Labour statistics. 1978-1998. OECD 1999.
Source: Yearbook of labour statistics 2001. International Labour Office. Geneva 2001. Labour force statistics. 1978-1998. OECD. 1999.

Table 10 – Standard age of entitlement to public old-age pensions, 1961-1995

Country	Males			Females		
	1961	1975	1995	1961	1975	1995
Western Europe						
Austria	65	65	65	60	60	60
Belgium	65	65	65	60	60	60
Denmark	67	67	67	67	67	67
Finland	65	65	65	65	65	65
France	65	65	60	65	65	60
Germany	65	65	65	65	65	65
Greece	65	62	62	60	57	57
Ireland	70	68	66	70	68	66
Italy	60	60	62	55	55	57
Netherlands	65	65	65	65	65	65
Norway	70	67	67	70	67	67
Portugal	65	65	65	65	62	62.5
Spain	65	65	65	65	65	65
Sweden	67	67	65	67	67	65
Switzerland	65	65	65	63	62	62
United Kingdom	65	65	65	60	60	60

Source: Blöndal S. and S. Scarpetta. 1999a. *The retirement decisions in OECD countries.* Economics Department Working Paper no. 202. OECD. Paris.

Table 11 – Standard age of entitlement to public old-age pensions in selected transition countries in the 1990s

Country	Year	Males	Females
Czech Republic	1995	60 (increase to 62 by 2006)	53-57* (increase to 57-61 by 2007)
Hungary	1997	62	57 (increase to 62 by 2009)
Poland	1998	65	60
Romania	2000	60 (increase to 65 by 2013)	57 (increase to 60 by 2013)
Slovak Republic	1988	60	53-56*
Estonia	1998	62.5 (increase to 63 by 2001)	57.5 (increase to 63 by 2016)
Latvia	2000	60 (increase to 62 by 2003)	57 (increase to 62 by 2005)
Lithuania	1994	61 (increase to 62.5 by 2009)	57 (increase to 60 by 2009)
Slovenia	2000	60 (increase to 63. minimum age 58)	53-58 (increase to 58-61. minimum age 58)

* depending on the number of children.
Source: E. Fultz and M. Ruck, Pension reform in central and eastern Europe: an update on the restructuring of national pension schemes in selected countries. International Labour Office. Central and eastern European team. Budapest 2001.

Table 12 – Employment rate of older workers in selected countries,[1] 1980-1999

Country	1980	1985	1990	1995	1999
Austria	...	...	...	29.0	29.2
Belgium	...	26.0	21.4	23.3	24.7
Denmark	...	50.1	53.6	49.3	54.2
Finland	47.1	45.4	42.6	34.4	39.2
France	50.7	37.2	35.6	33.5	34.2
Germany	42.2	35.5	36.8	37.5	38.5
Greece[2]	...	45.1	40.8	40.5	39.1
Ireland	...	40.9	38.6	39.2	43.7
Italy	...	33.3	32.0	27.0	27.5
Netherlands	36.3	27.3	22.4	22.7	35.3
Norway	63.9	65.5	61.8	63.1	67.3
Portugal	51.3	47.0	47.0	44.7	50.8
Spain	44.7	38.2	36.8	32.1	34.9
Sweden	65.7	65.0	69.4	61.9	64.0
Switzerland	...	...	...	69.8	71.7
United Kingdom	...	47.0	49.2	47.5	49.4

1. Employment of persons aged 55-64 as a percentage of the population aged 55-64.
2. The data refer to 1998.
Source: OECD Labour force statistics.

Table 13 – Employment rate of older workers in selected transition countries,[1] 1999-2000

Country	1999			2000		
	all	males	females	all	males	females
Central Europe						
Bulgaria	21.3	34.5	10.0	22.1	34.9	11.2
Czech Republic	37.6	53.2	23.6	36.1	51.6	22.1
Hungary	19.1	29.3	11.1	21.9	33.0	13.0
Poland	32.5	41.8	24.5	29.0	37.4	21.8
Romania	52.9	59.4	47.3	52.0	57.4	47.3
Slovak Republic	22.2	36.4	10.6	21.5	35.2	10.2
Baltic countries						
Estonia	47.9	59.2	39.3	43.0	50.2	37.5
Latvia	36.6	50.3	26.4	35.4	48.3	25.9
Lithuania	42.6	56.7	31.8	42.2	52.2	34.5
Other						
Slovenia	23.4	32.2	14.9	22.3	31.0	14.3

1. Employment of persons aged 55-64 as a percentage of the population aged 55-64.
Source: Employment and labour market in central European countries. no.3. 2001. European Commission, Eurostat.

Table 14 – Unemployment rates and the incidence of long-term unemployment, 1999

Country	Unemployment rate (percentage of labour force)		Unemployed for twelve months or more (percentage of unemployment)	
	15-64	45-64	15-64	45-64
Austria	4.7	4.7	31.7	46.4
Belgium	8.7	6.5	60.5	75.3
Denmark	5.2	4.4	20.2	33.4
Finland	10.3	8.3	28.4	45.6
France	12.1	8.5	38.6	58.3
Germany	8.9	10.6	50.8	61.7
Greece[1]	...	4.8	54.4	56.4
Ireland	5.9	5.1	...	...
Italy	11.8	4.7	60.6	61.6
Netherlands	3.6	2.6	37.7	58.5
Norway	3.2	1.3	6.8	9.1
Portugal	4.9	7.9	40.8	7.2
Spain	15.9	9.8	49.9	60.4
Sweden	7.1	5.5	30.1	47.1
Switzerland	3.2	2.4	34.4	54.5
United Kingdom	6.2	4.6	29.7	43.4
Central Europe				
Czech Republic	8.7	6.0	36.0	43.9
Hungary	7.0	4.4	49.3	58.0
Poland	12.6	7.9	41.6	47.4
Unweighted averages				
European Union	7.2	5.4	37.7	49.2

1. Data refer to 1998.
Source: OECD Unemployment duration and labour force databases.

Table 15 – Unemployment rates and the incidence of long-term unemployment in selected transition countries, 2000

Country	Unemployment rate (percentage of labour force)		Unemployed for twelve months or more (percentage of unemployment)	
	15-64	55-64	15-64	55-64
Central Europe				
Bulgaria	16.4	12.2	58.7	66.0
Czech Republic	8.8	5.3	50.0	43.9
Hungary	6.6	3.1	47.9	57.4*
Poland	16.6	9.7	54.6	51.8
Romania	7.7	1.1	49.2	59.9
Slovak Republic	19.1	12.7	54.6	59.5
Baltic countries				
Estonia	13.5	8.2	47.2	35.1*
Latvia	14.4	9.4	55.8	56.2
Lithuania	15.9	9.2	52.4	51.3*
Other				
Slovenia	7.1	6.1	62.7	84.3*

*based on the small size sample.
Source: Employment and labour market in central European countries. no.2 and 3. 2001. European Commission, Eurostat.

Table 16 – Expected old-age gross pension replacement rates: a summary indicator[1]

Country	1961	1975	1995
Western Europe			
Austria	79.5	79.5	79.5
Belgium	72.6	70.5	67.5
Denmark	35.9	42.3	56.2
Finland	34.9	58.6	60.0
France	50.0	62.5	64.8
Germany	60.2	59.6	55.0
Greece	...	...	120.0
Ireland	38.6	28.9	39.7
Italy	60.0	62.0	80.0
Netherlands	32.2	48.0	45.8
Norway	25.3	61.2	60.0
Portugal	85.0	77.0	82.6
Spain	...	...	100.0
Sweden	53.8	77.1	74.4
Switzerland	28.4	51.7	49.3
United Kingdom	33.4	33.8	49.8
Central and eastern Europe			
Czech Republic	...	...	53.2
Hungary	...	...	54.6
Poland	...	...	53.7

1. The figures refer to theoretical replacement rates and are based on several assumptions listed in the text. Details of the calculations can be found in Blöndal and Scarpetta (1999a).
Source: Blöndal S.and S. Scarpetta. 1999b. *Early retirement in OECD countries: the role of social security systems.* OECD Economic studies no. 29. OECD.Paris.

Table 17 – Expected increase in old-age pensions for a 55 year-old male by working for ten more years[1]

Percentage point increase in the summary replacement rate.

Country	1967	1995
Western Europe		
Austria	13	12
Belgium	32	15
Denmark	2	1
Finland	10	4
France	25	17
Germany	13	11
Greece	...	25
Ireland	0	0
Italy	24	10
Netherlands	0	0
Norway	17	9
Portugal	15	10
Spain	0	0
Sweden	21	0
Switzerland	12	11
United Kingdom	0	10
Central and eastern Europe		
Czech Republic	...	1
Hungary	...	1
Poland	...	9

1. It is assumed that the individual started work at the age of 20 so he has a potential contribution period of 35 years at the age of 55.
Source: Blöndal. S. and S. Scarpetta. 1999b. *Early retirement in OECD countries: the role of social security systems.* OECD Economic studies no. 29. OECD. Paris.

Table 18 – Pension contribution rates

Percent of average earnings.

Country	1967	1995
Austria	16.5	22.8
Belgium	12.5	16.4
Denmark	1.0	1.0
Finland	6.5	17.9
France	8.5	19.8
Germany	14	18.6
Ireland	5.2	15.7
Italy	15.8	29.6
Netherlands	10.2	14.5
Norway	12.8	22
Portugal	13.5	13.9
Spain	16	28.3
Sweden	6.4	19.8
Switzerland	4.0	8.4
United Kingdom	6.5	13.9

Source: Blöndal.S. and S.Scarpetta. 1999b. *Early Retirement in OECD Countries: the Role of Social Security Systems.* OECD Economic Studies no. 29. OECD. Paris.

Table 19 – Average implicit tax rate on continued work due to the old-age pension system, 1967 and 1995

Country	Postponing retirement from 55 to 64		Postponing retirement from 55 to 69	
	1967	1995	1967	1995
Austria	31	34	43	47
Belgium	-2	23	15	33
Denmark	0	0	4	5
Finland	0	22	9	33
France	2	14	8	42
Germany	4	14	19	23
Ireland	5	14	4	17
Italy	30	79	30	79
Netherlands	9	13	12	14
Norway	3	15	2	22
Portugal	5	4	25	25
Sweden	-9	18	0	22
Switzerland	-2	0	5	10
United Kingdom	6	5	9	10

Source: Blöndal S.and S. Scarpetta. 1999b, *Early retirement in OECD countries: the role of social security systems.* OECD Economic studies no. 29. OECD. Paris.

Table 20 – Replacement rates for older workers from non-employment benefit schemes in selected OECD countries, 1995

Yearly average from age 55 to the standard entitlement age for old-age pensions			
Country	Disability schemes	Unemployment schemes	Special ER schemes
Western Europe			
Austria	68.1	34.0	
Belgium	58.3	40.0	52.9
Denmark	38.8	71.5	20.0
Finland	60.0	30.0	
France	50.0	34.4	52.0
Germany	44.1	29.1	
Ireland	32.2	24.0	
Italy	60.0	50.0	70.0
Netherlands	70.0	52.5	
Norway	57.0		14.7
Portugal	71.7	35.9	
Spain	71.5	37.1	
Sweden	69.6		
United Kingdom		8.2	
Central and eastern Europe			
Czech Republic	44.7	5.6	
Hungary	55.8	18.6	
Poland	46.9	16.2	

Source: Blöndal S. and S. Scarpetta. 1999b. *Early retirement in OECD countries: the role of social security systems.* OECD Economic studies no. 29. OECD. Paris.

The authors

Dr Rossella Palomba is head of the Department on Family and Society at the National Institute for Population Research and Social Policy in Rome.

Address:
Institute for Population Research, Via Nizza 128, 00198 ROMA, Italy; tel.: (39) 06-4993-2844 ; e-mail: Palomba@irp.rm.cnr.it

Professor Irena E. Kotowska is the head of the Demographic Unit at the Institute of Statistics and Demography, Warsaw School of Economics.

Address:
Institute of Statistics and Demography, Warsaw School of Economics, Al. Niepodległości 162, 02-554 WARSAW, Poland; tel./fax: (48-22) 6466138; e-mail: iekoto@sgh.waw.pl

Titles in the same collection

24. **Information and education in demography**
Rossella Palomba, Alessandra Righi (1993)
(ISBN 92-871-2111-7)

25. **Political and demographic aspects of migration flows to Europe**
Raimondo Cagiano de Azevedo (editor) (1993)
(ISBN 92-871-2360-8)

26. **The future of Europe's population**
Robert Cliquet (editor) (1993)
(ISBN 92-871-2369-1)

27. **The demographic situation of Hungary in Europe**
Andras Klinger (1993)
(ISBN 92-871-2352-7)

28. **Migration and development cooperation**
Raimondo Cagiano de Azevedo (editor) (1994)
(ISBN 92-871-2611-9)

29. **Ageing and its consequences for the socio-medical system**
Jenny De Jong-Gierveld, Hanna Van Solinge (1995)
(ISBN 92-871-2685-2)

30. **The demographic characteristics of national minorities in certain European states (Volume 1)**
Werner Haug, Youssef Courbage, Paul Compton (1998)
(ISBN 92-871-3769-2)

31. **The demographic characteristics of national minorities in certain European states (Volume 2)**
Various authors (2000)
(ISBN 92-871-4159-2)

32. **International migration and regional population dynamics in Europe : a synthesis**
Philip Rees, Marek Kupiszewski (1999)
(ISBN 92-871-3923-7)

33. **Europe's population and labour market beyond 2000**
(Volume 1 : An assessment of trends and policy issues)
Aidan Punch, David L. Pearce (editors) (2000)
(ISBN 92-871-4273-4)

34. **Europe's population and labour market beyond 2000**
(Volume 2 : Country case studies)
Aidan Punch, David L. Pearce (editors) (2000)
(ISBN 92-871-4399-4)

35. **Fertility and new types of households and family formation in Europe**
Antonella Pinnelli, Hans Joachim Hoffmann-Nowotny and Beat Fux (2001)
(ISBN 92-871-4698-5)

36. **Trends in mortality and differential mortality**
Jacques Vallin and France Mesle, Tapani Valkonen (2001)
(ISBN 92-871-4725-6)

37. **People, demography and social exclusion**
Dragana Avramov (2002)
(ISBN 92-8715095-8)

38. **The demographic characteristics of immigrant populations**
Werner Haug, Paul Compton, Youssef Courbage (editors) (2002)
(ISBN 92-871-4974-7)

39. **Demographic consequences of economic transition in countries of central and eastern Europe**
Dimiter Philipov and Jürgen Dorbritz (2003)
(ISBN 92-871-5172-5)